25 Bicycle Tours in MAINE

Coastal and Inland Rides from Kittery to Caribou

Howard Stone

Second Edition

Backcountry Publications, Inc.   Woodstock, Vermont

An Invitation to the Reader

Although it is unlikely that the roads you cycle on these tours will change much with time, some road signs, landmarks and other items may. If you find that changes have occurred on these routes, please let us know so we may correct them in future editions. The author and publisher also welcome other comments and suggestions. Address all correspondence:

Editor, *Bicycle Tours*
Backcountry Publications, Inc.
P.O. Box 175
Woodstock, Vermont 05091

Library of Congress Cataloging-in-Publication Data

Stone, Howard, 1947–
    25 bicycle tours in Maine: coastal and inland rides
from Kittery to Caribou / by Howard Stone. —2nd ed.

    p.   cm.
    Includes bibliographical references.
    ISBN 0–88150–170–0 :
    1. Bicycle touring—Maine- —Guide-books. 2. Maine—
Description and travel—1981—Guide-books.
    I. Title II. Title: Twenty-five bicycle tours in Maine.
GV1045.5.M2S76   1990   89–78407
796.6'4'09741—dc20   CIP

Second edition, 1990. Fifth printing, 1995, updated
Published by Backcountry Publications
A division of The Countryman Press, Inc.
Woodstock, VT 05091

Text and cover design by Richard Widhu
Maps by Richard Widhu, © 1986 Backcountry Publications
Photographs by the author

Acknowledgements

I'd like to give special thanks to those people who accompanied me while I researched the book, often enduring days that began and ended at 3 a.m. In alphabetical order, they are Becky Burns, June Comeau, Leesa Mann, Dick Oliveira, Carla Petersen, and Gayle Yarrington. Gayle also helped me proofread the manuscript. Kevin and Anita Clifford allowed me to stay overnight numerous times, even though they had a newborn baby to take care of.

I would like to express my thanks to Donald Bumpus, of the Maine State Development Office—Division of Tourism, for offering me use of the department's photo collection. And to John Wojtowicz, who developed my photographs.

I am grateful to Chris Lloyd of Backcountry Publications and to Sarah Spiers, my editor, for their continued encouragement and support.

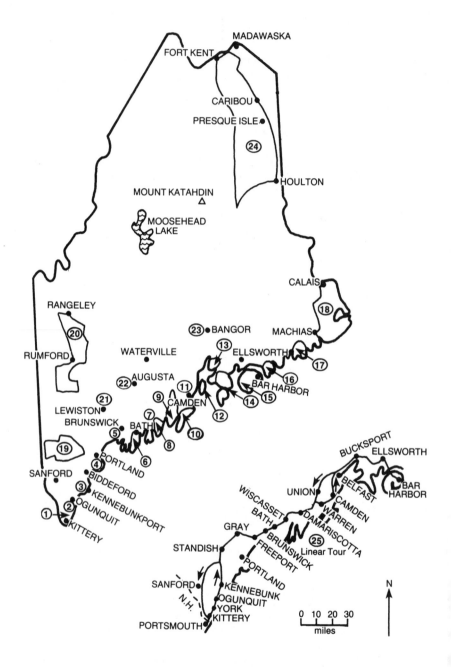

Contents

A back road stretches to the horizon across potato farms near Presque Isle.

Introduction

Maine offers thousands of miles of safe and scenic bicycling. The state is blessed with an impressive network of secondary roads, most of them paved but not heavily traveled. Away from busy arteries like Interstate 95 and Route 1, an unspoiled landscape of weathered fishing villages, rolling farmland, and elegant New England towns beckons the cyclist. Most of Maine is rural enough to give the cyclist a sense of remoteness and serenity, but the nearest town, village, or grocery store is usually not more than a few miles away.

About the Rides

Ideally a bicycle ride should be a scenic, relaxing, and enjoyable experience that brings you into intimate contact with the landscape. In striving to achieve this goal, I've routed the rides along paved secondary and rural roads to avoid busy highways as much as possible. The tours include scenic spots such as dams, falls, ponds, ocean views, open vistas and attractive villages.

Most of the rides fall between 25 and 45 miles in length, and a few have shorter or longer options. You can shorten any of the tours by examining the map and picking an alternative route. All the rides make a loop or figure eight rather than going out and then backtracking along the same road. I've included five overnight trips which average 40 to 55 miles per day. The last ride is a continuous linear tour from the southern tip of Maine to Bar Harbor and back.

If you've never ridden any distance, the thought of riding 25 or, heaven forbid, 50 miles may sound intimidating or even impossible. I want to emphasize, however, that anyone in normal health can do it—and enjoy it—if you get into a little bit of shape first, which you can accomplish painlessly by riding at a leisurely pace for an hour or two several times a week for about three weeks. At a moderate pace, you'll ride about ten miles per hour. If you think of the rides by the hour rather than by the mile, the numbers are much less intimidating.

Not counting long stops, a 25-mile ride should take about three hours at a leisurely speed and a 50-mile ride about six hours. However, I recommend that you start early and allow a full day for even the shorter rides because of the wealth of things to see and do along the way.

With the exception of the southern and extreme eastern coastal areas, Maine is rolling or hilly. As a result, biking the state involves some effort. Most of the rides ascend at least one or two hills, sometimes steep or long enough so that you will want to walk them. To compensate, however, there's a downhill run for every uphill climb. Except for a few difficult climbs in the northern and western parts of the state, no hills are long enough to be really discouraging. Most of the hills that you'll encounter are under a half mile long, with the steepest portion limited to a couple hundred yards or less.

It is obviously impossible to cover every scenic, historic, or popular spot in an area as large as Maine with only 25 rides, so some well-known places are not represented in the book. Old Orchard is a fine beach and amusement area, but it is neither very safe nor scenic for bicycling. Portland's museums, architectural landmarks, and waterfront shops are best visited on foot. South Harpswell and Bailey Island are lovely, but bicycling to them involves extensive backtracking. To get to Boothbay Harbor you have to either ride at least a few miles on Route 27, a busy and unattractive road, or follow secondary roads from Damariscotta and then backtrack along the same route. The Moosehead Lake, Allagash, and Mount Katahdin areas are spectacular, but bicycling in this part of Maine involves riding for long distances on dirt roads with an entourage of lumber trucks and large recreational vehicles. With the exception of Islesboro, Maine's numerous islands either are too small to warrant inclusion in the book, or, surprisingly, they don't have many views of the water from the roads.

Helpful Hints

1. If you've never ridden any distance, start with a short, easy tour, and work your way up to the more difficult ones.

2. Adjust your seat to the proper height and make sure that it is level. With your pedals at six and twelve o'clock, put the balls of your feet directly over the spindles. Your extended leg should be slightly bent. Then put both heels on the pedals. Your extended leg should now be straight, and you should be able to backpedal without rocking your fanny from side to side. If it rocks, the seat is too high; if your extended leg is still bent with the pedal at its lowest point, the seat is too low.

3. Pedal with the balls of your feet, not your arches or heels. Toe clips are ideal for keeping your feet in the proper position on the pedals; they also give you added leverage when going uphill. The straps should be *loose* so that you can take your feet off the pedals effortlessly.

4. Spin your legs quickly in your lower and middle gears, rather than grind along slowly in your higher ones. Using low gears is much more efficient and less tiring. Get used to riding at 70 revolutions per minute; then work your way up to above 80. If you find yourself pedaling below 70 RPM's, shift to a lower gear. To count your RPM's, use a watch with a second hand or, even better, a bicycle computer which measures cadence.

5. When approaching a hill, always shift into low gear *before* the hill,

not after you start climbing it. If it's a steep or long hill, get into your lowest gear right away. I use a fairly low gear even on moderate hills.

6. If you have a 10- or 12-speed bike, you'll find it much easier to climb hills if you get a freewheel (the rear cluster of gears) that goes up to 34 teeth instead of the standard 28 teeth. (You may have to buy a new rear derailleur to accommodate the larger shifts.) For the ultimate in hill-climbing ease, convert your bike to 15, 18, or 21 speeds, or buy a new one with this gearing.

7. Eat before you get hungry, drink before you get thirsty, and rest before you get tired.

8. To keep your pants out of your chain, tuck them inside your socks.

9. Don't wear jeans or cut-offs; their thick seams are uncomfortable.

About the Points of Interest

Maine has a wealth of museums and historic sites. I have intentionally not listed their hours and fees because they are subject to change, often from one year to the next. Most of Maine's attractions are open only during the summer or, with luck, between May and October. Many of the historic houses and smaller museums are open only two or three days a week because they depend on voluntary contributions and effort. If you really want to visit a site, phone before the ride to find out the hours.

As you pedal through towns and villages, try to notice each building. Maine's communities abound with nineteenth-century architecture, including elegant wooden houses, Victorian commercial buildings, stately white churches, inviting brick or stone libraries, and bell-towered schoolhouses.

About the Overnight Tours

An overnight tour requires some preparation. It is important to reserve your accommodations at least a week in advance—it's no fun to pull into town at dusk and find that all the motels are full. When you reserve the place where you'll be staying the night before the tour, mention that you will be taking a bicycle trip and leaving your car there for a few days.

Clothing and Equipment You will also need some extra equipment and clothing. It is essential to have a rear rack that sits above the back wheel, and a pair of panniers that clip onto the rack. Be sure to bring raingear; the most effective is made of Gore-tex®, a breathable synthetic fabric. (Many cyclists prefer a rain cape, which maximizes ventilation.) Bring an extra change of clothing and keep it in a closed plastic garbage bag, since even "water-repellent" panniers will leak in a heavy downpour. Wool clothing—or, even better, polypropylene—stays warm when wet, whereas cotton becomes cold and clammy, which can bring on hypothermia if the temperature is below 60 degrees. Don't forget a jacket; inland Maine can be chilly in the morning even during the summer. Bring an extra waterbottle, inner tube, brake cable, derailleur cable, and a few spare spokes (with nipples) fitted to your wheel. You should also bring a few additional tools (see **What to Bring With You**, #4).

Be sure that your bicycle is in good condition. Replace worn tires, tubes, and cables *before* the tour—if you break down in Aroostook County or the western mountains, there won't be a bike shop around the corner.

About the Maps

The maps are reasonably accurate, but I have not attempted to draw them strictly to scale. Congested areas may be enlarged in relation to the rest of the map for the sake of legibility. All the maps contain these conventions:

1. Highway numbers are circled; distances between intersections are not circled. If a section of road contains several intersections, small dots indicate the points between which an indicated distance applies.

2. Small arrows alongside the route indicate the direction of travel.

Safety

You will reduce your chances of having an accident by following these safety tips:

1. Ride on the right, with the traffic. Never ride against traffic.

2. Wear a helmet. Using a helmet is analagous to wearing a seat belt in a car. Most bicycle helmets are light, comfortable, and well-ventilated. In addition to cushioning your head after a fall, a helmet also provides protection from the sun and the rain.

3. Be sure your bike is mechanically sound. Its condition is especially important if you bought the bike at a discount store, where it was probably assembled by an amateur with little training. Above all, be sure that the wheels are secure and the brakes work.

4. Use a rear-view mirror. When you come to an obstacle—a pothole or a patch of broken glass—you can tell at a glance, without peeking back over your shoulder, whether or not it's safe to swing out into the road to avoid it. On narrow or winding roads you can always be aware of the traffic behind you and plan accordingly. Mirrors attach to either your helmet, your eyeglasses, or the end of your handlebars.

5. Stop signs and traffic lights are there for a reason—obey them.

6. Pay attention to the road surface. Not all roads in Maine are silk-smooth. Often the bicyclist must contend with bumps, ruts, cracks, potholes, and fish-scale sections of road that have been patched and repatched numerous times. When the road is rough, slow down and keep alert, especially going downhill. On bumps, you can relieve some of the shock by getting up off the seat.

7. If bicycling in a group, ride single file and at least 20 feet apart.

8. Use hand signals when turning. To signal a right turn, stick out your right arm.

9. If you stop to rest or examine your bike, pull it *completely* off the road.

10. Bring reflective legbands and a light with you in case you are caught in the dark. I like ankle lights; they're lightweight and bob up and down as you pedal for additional visibility.

11. Sleek black bicycle clothing is stylish, but bright colors are more visible.

12. Watch out for sand patches, which often build up at intersections, sharp curves, and the bottom of hills. Sand is very unstable if you're turning, so slow way down, stop pedaling, and steer in a straight line until you're beyond the sandy spot.

13. Avoid storm sewers with grates parallel to the roadway.

14. NEVER ride diagonally across railroad tracks—it is too easy to catch your wheel in the slot between the rails and fall. Either walk your bike across, or, if no traffic is in sight, cross the tracks at right angles by swerving into the road. When riding across tracks, slow down and get up off the seat to relieve the shock of the bump.

15. In towns, beware of car doors opening into your path. To be safe, any time you ride past a line of parked cars, stay four or five feet away from them. A car pulling to the side of the road in front of you is an obvious candidate for trouble.

16. Freshly oiled and sanded roads (it's done to seal cracks before winter) are treacherous and the only safe course is to slow down. If the oil is still wet or the sand is deep, walk.

17. A low sun limits the visibility of drivers, especially those peering through a smeared or dirty windshield. Assume that anyone driving into a low sun may not see you, and give these cars the benefit of the doubt at intersections. Use your rear-view mirror to monitor the traffic behind you if you're pedaling directly into the sun.

18. Little kids riding their bikes in circles in the middle of the road or shooting in and out of driveways aren't expecting you. Call out "Beep-beep" or "Watch out" as you approach.

19. In the fall, wet leaves are very slippery. Avoid turning on them.

20. If a dog chases you, try to outrun it—often you can, because most dogs are territorial and will only chase you a short distance. Spin your legs quickly; it is hard for a dog to bite a fast-rotating target. If you can't outrun the animal, use dog repellent, or dismount and walk with your bike between you and the dog. Never swerve into the middle of the road or ride on the left to avoid a dog. Often, yelling "Stay!" or "No!" in an authoritative voice will make a dog back off.

What to Bring with You

You will enjoy the tours more if you add a few basic accessories to your bike and bring a few items with you.

1. **Bike rack.** It's so much easier to whip your bike on and off a rack than to wrestle it into and out of your car or trunk. I prefer bike racks that attach to the back of the car—do you really want to hoist your bike over your head onto the roof? If you use a rack that fits onto the back of the car, make sure that the bike is at least a foot off the ground and that the bicycle tire is well above the tailpipe. Hot exhaust blows out tires!*

2. **Handlebar bag with transparent map pocket on top.** It's always helpful to have some carrying capacity on your bike. Most handlebar bags are large enough to hold tools, a lunch, or even a light jacket. It is easy to follow the route if the map or directions are readily visible in the map pocket. For additional carrying capacity, you can buy a metal rack that fits above the rear wheel and a pack that fits on top of the rack.

Always carry things on your bike, not on your back. A knapsack raises your center of gravity and makes you more unstable; it also digs painfully into your shoulders if you have more than a couple of pounds in it.

3. **Waterbottle.** On any ride of more than fifteen miles you will be thirsty. If it's a hot day, or on the overnight tours, bring two waterbottles.

4. **Basic tools.** Tire irons, a six-inch adjustable wrench, a small pair of pliers, a small standard screwdriver, and a small Phillips-head screwdriver are all you need to take care of virtually all roadside emergencies. A rag (or packaged moist towelettes) and a tube of hand cleaner are useful if you have to handle your chain. On the overnight tours, it's a good idea to bring a few extra tools: a freewheel remover (make sure it fits your freewheel; there are different models), a chain rivet remover, a spoke wrench, a crank tool to tighten your crank bolt should it become loose (make sure it's the right size) and Allen wrenches to fit any Allen nuts on your bike.** On the overnight tours, also bring a spare brake cable, a spare derailleur cable, and a few extra spokes and spoke nipples (be sure that the spokes fit your wheel). I tape the extra spokes to my pump.

5. **Pump and spare tube.** If you get a flat, you're immobilized unless you can pump up a new tube or patch the old one. On the road, it is easier to install a new tube than to patch the old one. Do the patching at home. Pump up the tire until it's hard, and you are on your way.

If you cycle a lot, you will get flats—it's a fact of life. Most flats are on the rear tire, because that's where most of your weight is. You should therefore practice taking the rear wheel off and putting it back on the bike, and taking the tire off and placing it back on the rim, until you can do it

*My thanks to Pam Jones for suggesting this.

**Allen nuts have a small hexagonal socket on top. They are loosened and tightened with an L-shaped wrench that fits snugly into the socket.

confidently. It's much easier to practice at home than to fumble by the roadside.

6. **Dog repellent.** When you ride in rural areas you will occasionally be chased by dogs. The best repellent is a commercial product called Halt, an extract of hot peppers that comes in a small aerosol can and is available in many bike shops. You also may be able to obtain it from your post office (many mail carriers use it) or from the manufacturer, Animal Repellents, Inc., Griffin, GA 30223. Another alternative is to carry an ammonia-filled squirt gun or small plant sprayer. Just make sure that the container doesn't leak. Repellent is effective only if you can grab it instantly when you need it—don't put it in your handlebar pack, a deep

The Sandy River plunges over Smalls Falls, near Madrid.

pocket, or any place else where you'll have to fish around for it. I clip Halt to the top of my handlebar pack.

7. **Fenders.** When the roads are wet, fenders prevent a plume of water and mud from streaming up your back and gumming up your brakes and front derailleur.

8. **Bicycle computer or odometer.** A bicycle computer is the best device to indicate distance traveled. Computers are very easy to read because they sit on top of your stem and have large, clear digits. Most computers indicate not only distance, but also speed, elapsed time, and cadence. They have dropped in price in the last few years, and most cost about $50 or $60. I like the solar-powered model.

A poor cousin to the computer is the traditional odometer, which is harder to read because it is mounted on the hub instead of the stem, and the digits are small. Odometers also are not as accurate because, unlike computers, they cannot be calibrated to the exact circumference of your tire.

9. **Bike lock.** Common sense dictates locking your bicycle if you leave it unattended. The best locks are the rigid, boltcutter-proof ones like Kryptonite® or Citadel®. The next best choice is a strong cable that cannot be quickly severed by a normal-sized boltcutter or hacksaw.

10. **Food.** Always bring some food with you when you go for a ride. Some of the rides go through remote areas with many miles between places to buy food, and that country store you were counting on may be closed on weekends or out of business. Fruit is nourishing and contains a lot of water. A couple of candy bars or pieces of pastry will provide a burst of energy for the last ten miles if you are getting tired. (Don't eat sweets before then—the energy burst lasts only about an hour, then your blood sugar level drops to below where it was earlier and you'll be really weak.)

For liquids, the best choice is plain old water, and the worst choice is carbonated beverages. Fruit juice is fine in conjunction with water.

11. **Helmet.** See **Safety**, #2.

12. **Rear-view mirror.** See **Safety**, #4.

13. **Bicycle lights and reflective legbands.** See **Safety**, #10.

14. **Bicycling gloves.** Gloves designed for biking, with padded palms and no fingers, will cushion your hands and protect them if you fall. For maximum comfort, use handlebar padding also.

15. **Toe clips.** See **Helpful Hints**, #3.

16. **Roll of electrical tape.** You never know when you'll need it.

Using the Maps and Directions

Unfortunately, a book format does not lend itself to quick and easy consultation while you're on your bike. The rides will go more smoothly if you don't have to dismount at each intersection to consult the map or directions. You can solve this problem by making a photocopy of the directions to carry in your map pocket. You will have to dismount occasionally to turn the sheet over or to switch sheets, but most people find it easier to follow the directions than the map.

In the directions, I have indicated the names of roads if there was a street sign at the time I researched the route, and I did not indicate the name of the road if the street sign was absent. Street signs may appear or disappear at any time, and the name of a road may change.

The directions indicate the distance to the next turn or major intersection, so it will be very helpful to have a bicycle computer or an odometer. Each direction begins with the cumulative mileage that you have covered up to that point. The cumulation is meant to be only a guideline. No two computers or odometers are calibrated exactly the same, so most likely there will be a discrepancy between the cumulated mileages in the book and the reading on your own computer or odometer. The longer the ride, the greater the discrepancy will be.

In writing the directions, it is obviously not practical to mention every single intersection. Always stay on the main road unless the directions state otherwise.

In addition to distances and a description of the next intersection, the directions also mention points of interest and situations that require caution. Any hazardous spot, for example an unusually busy intersection or bumpy section of road, has been clearly indicated by a **Caution** warning. It's a good idea to read over the entire tour before taking it, in order to familiarize yourself with the terrain, points of interest, and places requiring caution.

In the directions, certain words occur frequently, so let me define them to avoid any confusion.

To ''bear'' means to turn diagonally, at an angle between a right-angle turn and going straight ahead. In these illustrations, you bear from road A onto road B.

To ''merge'' means to come into a road diagonally, or even head-on, if a side road comes into a main road. In the examples, road A merges into road B.

To turn "sharply" means to turn at an angle greater than 90 degrees, in other words, to make a hairpin or other very sharp turn. In the examples, you turn sharply from road A onto road B.

Bicycle Clubs

If you would like to bike with a group and meet other people who enjoy bicycling, join a bicycle club. Most clubs have weekend rides of comfortable length, with a shortcut if you don't want to ride too far. Some clubs hand out maps or directions before the ride, or mark the route by painting arrows in the road at the turns. The largest club in Maine is the Penobscot Wheelmen, RR2, Box 703, Augusta, ME 04330. Other clubs: Casco Bay Bicycle Club, 37 Bernadette Street, Westbrook, ME 04092. M.W.B.C., 9 Bickford Avenue, Brunswick, ME 04011. Maine Wheels, 225 Paris Hill Road, South Paris, ME 04281. The County Pedalers, 45 Second Street, Presque Isle, ME 04769. These clubs are affiliated with the League of American Bicyclists, the main national organization of and for bicyclists. The League has an excellent monthly magazine and a dynamic legislative action program. Its address is 190 West Ostend Street, Suite 120, Baltimore, MD 21230-3755.

Many bicycle shops run informal group rides. Ask your local shop if it runs any, or if any other shops in the area do. If there is no club within an hour's drive, consider starting one!

Further Reading and Resources

The Maine Atlas and Gazetteer. DeLorme Publishing Company, Freeport, ME, 1995. This is a superb resource that is updated every year. It divides the entire state into seventy quadrangles, each at a scale of two miles to the inch. This scale is large enough to show every back road, lake, stream, and most points of interest. In addition to the maps, the atlas contains lists and brief descriptions of beaches, nature preserves, parks, hiking trails, unique natural areas, waterfalls, canoe trips, ski areas, lighthouses, museums, historic sites, country inns, and campgrounds.

Maine: An Explorer's Guide, by Christina Tree. Seventh Edition. Countryman Press, Woodstock, VT, 1994. This is the best guidebook to the state in print. It describes points of interest, recreational areas, cultural events, fairs and festivals, places to shop, lodging, and restaurants.

Bicycling. DeLorme Publishing Company, Freeport, ME, 1994. This pamphlet includes 23 maps that indicate suggested rides. It covers several areas not included in this book, including South Harpswell-Bailey Island, the Boothbay Harbor region, the islands of Vinalhaven and North

Haven, Ellsworth-Trenton-Lamoine, Bucksport-Bangor, Bangor-Orono-Old Town, the Belgrade Lakes region, Naples-Bridgton-Harrison, and others. There's even a Century (a hundred-mile ride) northeast of Augusta.

Greater Portland Bikeways, available from the Portland Chamber of Commerce, 142 Free Street, Portland, ME 04101. This map shows recommended roads for bicycling in the area bounded by Biddeford, Brunswick, and Sebago Lake, with a detailed map of Portland on the back. It was published in 1982.

Maine Coast: Down East Vacation Guide, by the editors of *Down East* Magazine. This guide is a newsstand publication which is revised annually. It describes things to see and do and has calendars of events for the different sections of Maine. It covers inland Maine as well as the coast.

Maine Geographic series. DeLorme Publishing Company, Freeport, ME, 1994. This series of pamphlets (**Bicycling** is one of them) covers numerous topics, including wildlife, historic sites, islands, lighthouses, natural sites, country inns, canoeing, and hiking.

Bed and Breakfast in New England, by Bernice Chesler. Fourth Edition. Globe Pequot Press, Chester, CT, 1994.

Recommended Country Inns, New England, by Elizabeth Squier. Fourteenth edition. Globe Pequot Press, Chester, CT, 1994.

The Southern Coast

2.

The Southern Beaches: York—Ogunquit

Distance: 27 miles
Terrain: Gently rolling, with two short hills.
Special features: Long Sands Beach, Short Sands Beach, Cape Neddick Light, Perkins Cove, Marginal Way.
Caution: Shore Road, between York Beach and Ogunquit, is very narrow, very winding, and heavily traveled on beach days. When this road is busy, it is difficult for traffic to pass a bicycle without either risking a head-on collision or squeezing the bicycle off the road. Please take this ride in the early morning or during the off-season.

The coastline between York and Ogunquit, about 10 to 15 miles north of Kittery, is the most southerly of Maine's major beach areas. Long Sands Beach and Ogunquit Beach are long and straight, stretching for several miles along the shore. Between the beaches are rockbound coves and headlands where cliffs and ledges plunge to the sea. Cape Neddick Light, Perkins Cove, and Marginal Way, a dramatic oceanfront footpath, are as scenic as any spots in Maine, and are fine examples of the images that spring to mind when you think of the phrase "Maine coast." In contrast, only three miles inland lies a completely different landscape of woods, ponds, soft green farms, and lonely country roads that hardly ever see a tourist.

Unless you specifically wish to go to the beach on a hot day, the ride is infinitely more enjoyable when the beaches are not in use. During the off-season, or early on summer mornings, you can gaze calmly at the broad sweep of Long Sands Beach without dodging car doors as they open into your path, and you can enjoy the charm of Perkins Cove without jockeying your bike through hordes of tourists. Shore Road, a delightful ride when not busy, will be nearly deserted, and when you arrive at Ogunquit you won't have to ride in the gutter because of the mile-long line of cars inching its way to the beach.

If you decide to go to the beach, brace yourself: the water is cold. Not just brisk or chilly or invigorating, but frigid, arctic, the temperature at which beer should be served. If you throw an ice cube into the ocean, it's a wonder that it melts. Even on a 90-degree day, only a hardy few will actually be swimming. I've always been somewhat mystified that people go to the Maine beaches at all. It's fortunate that they do, otherwise the traffic to Cape Cod would back up all the way to Boston.

Directions for the ride

Start from the town parking lot in York Village on Long Sands Road immediately north of Route 1A. To get there see the York-Eliot-Kittery ride (#1).

0.0 Turn left out of the parking lot and immediately left on Route 1A (**Caution** here).

To your right on Route 1A, a block away, is the York Village Historic District (see the York-Eliot-Kittery ride for more detail). It's worth visiting after the ride.

After 0.9 mile, Route 1A curves left and Harbor Beach Road bears right. Here the route stays on Route 1A , but if you bear right for 100 yards you'll come to a small beach cupped between two headlands. The elegant Stage Neck Inn commands the headland on your right. The community just before the intersection is York Harbor.

1.0 Continue on Route 1A for 0.6 mile to Norwood Farms Road on the right.

1.6 Turn right. After 0.3 mile, the main road curves sharply left. Continue for 0.6 mile to the end (Route 1A again).

2.5 Right for 2.2 miles to Nubble Road, which bears right uphill.

Caution: Watch for car doors opening into your path. The road hugs Long Sands Beach. On the left is an endless, congested row of beach houses. Cape Neddick rises ahead and to the right.

4.7 Bear right on Nubble Road, which heads out to Cape Neddick. After ½ mile the main road bears right, following the ocean. Continue on the main road for 0.4 mile to a fork where Sohier Park Road bears right.

Handsome, cedar-shingled houses perch on the low bluff overlooking the sea.

5.6 Bear right on Sohier Park Road for 0.1 mile to the dead end and Cape Neddick Light.

The lighthouse, also called Nubble Light, stands dramatically above a craggy ledge separated from the mainland by a narrow channel. Attached to the lighthouse is the white keeper's residence, and a small red outbuilding adds to the charm of this spot. The lighthouse was built in 1873.

5.7 From the lighthouse, backtrack 0.1 mile to the main road.

5.8 Right for 0.6 mile to Kendall Road on the right. It's after Forthill Avenue.

6.4 Right for ½ mile to the crossroads and stop sign.

Caution: There is a steep, curving downhill ride shortly after you turn. This is a beautiful narrow lane, with the rocky shore on the right and elegant wooden summer homes on the left.

6.9 Turn right at stop sign, following the ocean on your right, for 0.3 mile to the end (Route 1A), in the center of York Beach.

The road follows Short Sands Beach. Across from it is Ocean House, a rambling Victorian resort hotel. York Beach is cluttered with shops and snack bars: my favorite is the Goldenrod, a landmark since the turn of the century.

7.2   Right on Route 1A for 0.6 mile to a fork where Route 1A bears left and Shore Road goes straight.

7.8   Straight on Shore Road for 0.6 mile to Agamenticus Avenue, which bears right as you start to go uphill.

8.4   Bear right for 0.6 mile to the end (Shore Road again).

Agamenticus Avenue loops close to the coast, passing gracious wood and stone houses.

9.0   Right on Shore Road for 3.8 miles to a small road that turns sharply right at a stop sign and traffic island. The main road curves left here. A sign in the traffic island says "to Perkins Cove."

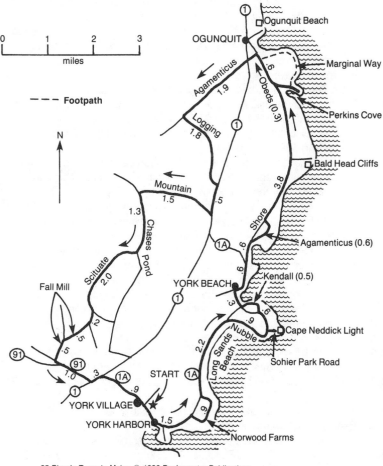

25 Bicycle Tours in Maine © 1986 Backcountry Publications

After 1.8 miles you'll see a graceful stone Episcopal church on the right at the top of a hill. Immediately after the church a road on the right leads 0.4 mile to Bald Head Cliffs, which rise vertically from the ocean to a height of about 60 feet. The Cliff House, a sprawling old resort, stretches along the top of the cliff.

12.8   Turn sharply right at the stop sign for 0.3 mile to the tip of the small peninsula bordering Perkins Cove.

Perkins Cove is a small inlet that is clogged with boats, spanned by a tall footbridge, and lined with a dense cluster of weathered fishing shacks that now house craft shops, restaurants, galleries, and artists' studios. Although commercial, the cove is picturesque, especially when it is not clogged with pedestrians and traffic.

A visit to Ogunquit is not complete without a stroll along Marginal Way, the mile-long footpath that hugs the rocky coastline from Perkins Cove almost to the center of town. Halfway down the road to the Cove, just before the narrow neck of land, the path begins on the left from the back of the parking lot. Lock your bike near the parking lot and savor the walk.

13.1   From Perkins Cove, backtrack 0.3 mile to Shore Road.

13.4   Bear right for 0.6 mile to Obeds Lane, a narrow lane on the left immediately before the Seacastles Resort on the left.

Shortly before the intersection, notice the elegant fieldstone library, built in 1897, on the left.

The loop route turns left on Obeds Lane, but if you'd like to visit Ogunquit Beach, continue straight for ¼ mile to the main square, and turn 90 degrees right for ¼ mile to the beach.

Einstein's, wedged into the triangle where Shore Road merges into Route 1, is a good lunch spot that serves genuine bagels (a great biking food) slathered with cream cheese.

14.0   Left on Obeds Lane for 0.3 mile to Route 1, at the traffic light.

14.3   Cross Route 1 onto Agamenticus Road (**Caution** here). Go 1.9 miles to an unmarked road on the left that goes down a steep little hill.

As soon as you cross Route 1, the traffic disappears. Agamenticus Road, and the next few roads on the ride, are winding and wooded.

16.2   Left for 1.8 miles to the end (Route 1).

18.0   Right for ½ mile to Mountain Road on the right.

18.5   Right for 1.5 miles to the end (Chases Pond Road on the left).

You'll cross over the Maine Turnpike just before the end.

20.0   Left on Chases Pond Road for 1.3 miles to a fork where Scituate Road bears right.

At the fork, Chases Pond is on the right.

21.3   Bear right, following the pond, for 2 miles to another fork.

You'll see Scituate Pond on the right ½ mile before the fork.

23.3   Bear right (still Scituate Road) for ¼ mile to another fork where Fall Mill Road bears right. It comes up while you're going downhill.

Cape Neddick Light, York (also called Nubble Light), was built in 1873.

23.6   Bear right on Fall Mill Road for ½ mile to the end, at the stop sign.

24.1   Left (still Fall Mill Road) for ½ mile to the end. You'll climb a short steep hill.

24.6   Turn left, and immediately merge head-on into Route 91 South. Go straight for 1 mile to the end (Route 1), at the stop sign.

        You'll enjoy an exhilarating downhill ride across large farms to an inlet, part of the York River.

25.6   Left on Route 1 for 0.3 mile to Route 1A, which bears right.

25.9   Bear right for 0.9 mile to Long Sands Road, which bears left in the center of York Village.

        Just before the intersection, you'll see the Historic District on the right, across from the splendid First Parish Church and the handsome granite library. The large red gambrel-roofed building next to the graveyard is the Old Gaol, built in 1719. It serves as the museum for the historic area.

26.8   Bear left on Long Sands Road and immediately right into the parking lot. Rick's All Season Restaurant and the Spice of Life, both at the intersection, are good lunch spots.

Bicycle Repair Services

Movin' On, 11 South Main Street, Ogunquit (646-2810)
Wheels & Waves, Route 1, Wells (646-5774)
Berger's Bike Shop, 241 York Street, York Village (363-4070)

3.

Kennebunk — Kennebunkport

Distance: 24 miles
Terrain: Fairly flat, with one short, steep hill.
Special features: Fine architecture in Kennebunk and Kennebunkport, Dock Square in Kennebunkport, George Bush's summer home, beaches and rocky coast, Seashore Trolley Museum.
Caution: During the summer, traffic along the coast is very heavy, especially in Dock Square and on Ocean Avenue, a narrow, curving road where it is difficult for a car to pass a bicycle safely. The best time to ride is early morning or during the off-season.
Important note: The route passes George Bush's summer home on Ocean Avenue. In general, bicycles are allowed to go through, even when the former President is in town. A security officer may tell you to proceed without stopping. However, the Secret Service may block the road at any time, for example when the former President is using the road or is outside the house. If this is the case, an alternative route is available.

The Kennebunk region, about midway between Kittery and Portland, contains a charming mixture of broad sandy beaches, rock-rimmed coves and headlands, and resort towns graced with 19th-century mansions and elegant beachfront hotels. During the summer, the coastal areas are jammed with traffic and pedestrians, but in the off-season they are refreshingly deserted. Just inland from the ocean, secondary roads abound that are relatively traffic-free even during midsummer.

The ride starts from Kennebunk, a small town which stretches from its traditional brick downtown area on Route 1 to the ocean about four miles southeast. In the center of town is the Brick Store Museum, a cluster of 19th-century mercantile buildings with exhibits of local history and the decorative arts. As you pedal east out of town on Route 35, you'll pass gracious homes from the Federal and Victorian eras, many topped with cupolas and widow's walks.

A secondary road leads from the edge of town to the ocean and then follows the shore along Kennebunk Beach, passing rambling cedar-shingled homes overlooking the water and also the Narragansett, an enormous Victorian hotel that now houses condominiums. This road suddenly turns inland along the Kennebunk River into Kennebunkport.

Kennebunkport is a lively, congested tourist mecca that is more attractive than most because it has not been despoiled by sterile new buildings, cutesy reproductions, tacky fast-food joints, or shantytowns of little beach cottages. The focal point of Kennebunkport is Dock Square, a compact nest of boutiques, antique shops, galleries, and small restaurants, all in original 18th- and 19th-century buildings. Within several blocks of the square are numerous fine homes, many of which are now inns, built during the early 1800s by prosperous merchants and shipbuilders.

The route heads south and then east from Dock Square along famed Ocean Avenue, which follows the east bank of the Kennebunk River for a short distance to its mouth and then hugs the open sea past rocky coves and headlands. The road passes several large summer hotels from the Victorian era that maintain their turn-of-the-century elegance and dozens of smaller inns housed in charming old buildings with wide porches and bay windows. Kennebunkport boasts the largest concentration of traditional inns and resort hotels in New England.

From Ocean Avenue it's a mile and a half to Cape Porpoise, an attractive village which is partly a summer colony and partly a fishing port, rimming a small harbor lined with docks and weathered fishermen's sheds. Beyond, the route turns inland on tranquil wooded roads with very little traffic.

After several miles you'll come to the Seashore Trolley Museum, which maintains a collection of trolleys and antique buses from around the world. It also has a comprehensive bookstore relating to the history of trolleys and railroads. Admission to the museum includes a 20-minute ride on one of several trolleys which have been maintained in operating condition, complete with a conductor in period costume. The museum runs entirely on volunteer effort.

From the trolley museum, it's two miles to the small crossroads village of Arundel, where you can stop at the Cape-Able Bike Shop, and another three miles back to Kennebunk. About a mile before the end you'll pass the town's best-known landmark, the Wedding Cake House. This architectural curiosity, built during the 1820s, is a yellow mansion that is encased to the point of grotesqueness with ornate gingerbread trim. According to legend, the house was built by a sea captain who was called to duty during his wedding reception, before he could present the wedding cake to his bride. When he returned, he added the scrollwork to make up for his untimely departure.

Directions for the ride

Start from the municipal parking lot in Kennebunk on the east side of Route 1, behind the commercial buildings in the center of town. The lot is at the corner of Route 1 and Grove Street, just south of Route 35. If this lot is full, there is another lot behind the buildings on the other side of Route 1.

0.0 Right on Route 1, heading north, for 0.2 mile to the traffic light (Route 35 on the left).

0.2 Straight for one block to another traffic light where Route 35 bears right.
The Brick Store Museum is on your right at the intersection.

0.2 Bear slightly right on Route 35 (Summer Street) for 0.7 mile to Sea Road on the right, shortly after a railroad bridge.

Notice the elegant homes along the road. The Taylor-Barry House, a Federal-style sea captain's mansion built in 1803 (at 24 Summer Street), is open to the public on weekday afternoons during the summer.

0.9 Right on Sea Road for 2.4 miles to the traffic light (Route 9).

3.3 Straight for 2.8 miles to the traffic light (Route 9 again).

After about a mile the road curves left along the ocean and follows Kennebunk Beach. After turning inland, you'll pass a Franciscan monastery on your right. It has an English Tudor main building, a vaulted stone shrine, and a footpath leading to the Kennebunk River.

6.1 Right on Route 9 for 0.3 mile to Dock Square, just after the bridge.

Caution: The metal-grate bridge is very slippery when wet. It's safest to walk your bike on the sidewalk and enjoy the view, pedestrian traffic permitting.

In Dock Square the ride turns right, but it's worth exploring the immediate area to appreciate its fine architecture. Just beyond the square is White Columns, a splendid Greek Revival mansion with its original furnishings, and the graceful Congregational Church at the

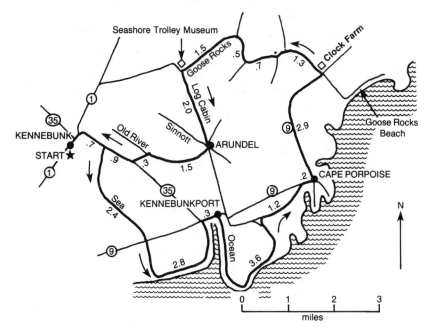

end of a side street. In Dock Square itself, the Book Port is a wonderful old bookstore where you can browse for hours.

6.4 In Dock Square turn right on Ocean Avenue, following the river on your right, for 3.6 miles to a road that bears right as you start to climb a steep, very short hill. If Ocean Avenue is blocked off in front of George Bush's summer home (after about 1.5 miles), backtrack to Dock Square. Turn right, and follow Route 9 about 2 miles to Cape Porpoise, where Route 9 turns left. (Route 9 jogs right and then left just past Dock Square.) Resume with mile **11.4**. **Caution:** Route 9 is busy and fairly narrow.

As soon as you turn onto Ocean Avenue, the side streets on the left are lined with handsome houses. After several blocks, you'll pass the finest of all, the Captain Lord Mansion, set back about 100 yards from the road at the head of a large lawn. It's a yellow Federal-style building, now an inn, with an octagonal cupola.

A mile from the square are three grand Victorian hotels, the Colony, The Nonantum, and the Breakwater. A short distance beyond, notice the fieldstone Episcopal church on the right, perched on the rocky shore. Shortly after the church is Walker Point; the road to it is blocked with "Restricted access" signs and a gatehouse. On the point is the summer estate of former President George Bush.*

Shortly before the intersection, a side road turns sharply right to the Shawmut Inn, another Victorian classic. Ahead, notice the small stone church on the left.

10.0 Bear right for 50 yards to the end, turn right, and go 1.2 miles to the end, at the stop sign (merge right on Route 9).

11.2 Bear right for 0.2 mile to the intersection where Route 9 turns left and a smaller road goes straight, in Cape Porpoise.

Bradbury Brothers Market, on your right at the intersection, is a wonderful old-fashioned country store. Here the loop route turns left on Route 9, but if you either go straight or turn right for 0.7 mile you'll hug the picturesque harbor. There's a seafood snack bar at the end of the road that goes straight.

11.4 Left on Route 9 East for 2.9 miles to a crossroads.

On the far left corner is the Clock Farm, an unusual house with a clock tower above the barn.

Side Trip: Here the ride turns left, but if you turn right for about a mile you'll come to Goose Rocks Beach, an attractive spot with the ocean on one side of the road and old wooden summer houses on the other. The beach is uncrowded because parking is very limited.

14.3 Left at the crossroads for 1.3 miles to a fork. Ignore the paved road on the right 0.2 mile before the fork.

---

*For a lighthearted account of the former President's presence in Kennebunkport, see *Bush Country, By George,* by Thistle McTavish and Allan Swenson. Portland, Maine: Guy Gannett Publishing Company, 1981. Ask for it at the Book Port.

15.6 Bear right for 0.7 mile to another fork where the main road bears right.

16.3 Bear right for ½ mile to another fork.

16.8 Bear left for 1.5 miles to the end.

    The Seashore Trolley Museum is on your right at the intersection, about 100 yards down the road.

18.3 Left at the end (if you visited the museum, turn left when you leave it) for 2 miles to a five-way intersection.

    This is the village of Arundel. The Cape-Able Bike Shop is a sharp left at the intersection, 100 yards behind the church.

20.3 Bear right opposite the cemetery (don't turn 90 degrees right opposite the church) for 1.5 miles to the second paved left.

21.8 Left for 0.3 mile to the end (merge right on Routes 9A and 35). You'll cross the Kennebunk River.

22.1 Bear right for 1.6 miles to the traffic light (Route 1).

    The Wedding Cake House is on the right after ½ mile.

23.7 Bear left at the light on Route 1. Just ahead is another light. Continue straight for 0.2 mile to Grove Street on the left.

23.9 Left and immediately right into the parking lot.

Bicycle Repair Services

Cape-Able Bike Shop, Arundel Road, Kennebunkport (967-4382)

The Clock Farm in Kennebunkport is one of the town's many fine nineteenth-century houses.

4.

Lighthouse Loop: Scarborough — Cape Elizabeth — South Portland

Distance: 31 miles (36 with side trip to Prouts Neck)
Terrain: Fairly flat, with two moderate hills.
Special features: Lighthouses, Crescent Beach, views of the Portland skyline.

The square peninsula that juts east from the Scarborough River to Cape Elizabeth, immediately south of Portland, provides pleasant and relaxed bicycling. The shoreline contains a varied mixture of salt marshes, gently curving beaches, craggy headlands, and busy port areas. Most of the region is suburban with well-spaced houses, landscaped grounds, and tree-lined streets. Even in South Portland, the most urban part of the region, the route follows residential side streets without much traffic. Along the southern and southwestern fringes, the suburban areas become almost rural, with tracts of woodland, expanses of farmland and large estates that sweep down to the water's edge.

The ride starts from Scarborough, a large township that extends from the rural farmland west of the Maine Turnpike to the ocean. As you head south toward the coast, you'll skirt the vast salt marshes surrounding the mouth of the Scarborough River. A side trip leads down the beach-lined promontory to Prouts Neck, a staid, private enclave where the well-to-do have summered for years. The route heads east to Cape Elizabeth, passing gentleman farms, country estates, and Crescent Beach State Park, which is the closest good beach to Portland.

In Cape Elizabeth the shoreline turns abruptly north and changes in character from flat and sandy to rugged and rocky. Cape Elizabeth is a wealthy community that commands most of the eastern shore of the peninsula, with fine houses and two picturesque lighthouses perched on the ledges above the ocean. Commanding the high headland where the coastline turns from east to north is Two Lights State Park, formerly a gun emplacement during World War II, with dramatic views and footpaths along the cliff tops. Just north of the park, at the peninsula's most easterly point, is Cape Elizabeth Light. Four miles north, guarding a spectacular rocky promontory, stands Portland Head Light, my favorite lighthouse in Maine. With its splendid setting in a large park, it is hard to believe that it is only four miles from Portland. The graceful white tower, built in 1791, is connected to a handsome keeper's dwelling with a peaked maroon roof.

On windy days, the waves crash with dramatic force against the adjoining ledges.

From Portland Head Light it's only three miles to Portland Harbor, at the northern tip of the peninsula in South Portland. From the shore are good views of the Portland skyline on the opposite shore. The return trip to Scarborough heads southwest on quiet side streets and then along secondary roads through a mostly wooded area.

Directions for the ride

Start from Oak Hill Plaza in Scarborough, on Route 114 just west of Route 1. If you are driving from Portland, cross the Route 1 bridge (at the end of St. John Street) into South Portland. Go about 5 miles to Route 114, at a traffic light. Turn right; the Plaza is just ahead on the right. If you are driving from the Maine Turnpike, get off at Exit 7. Bear right immediately after the toll booth (the sign says to Maine Mall Road). Turn left at the end of the exit ramp on Payne Road (Maine Mall Road is on the right). Go 0.8 mile to Route 114, at a traffic light. Turn left for about 2 miles to Oak Hill Plaza on the left, just before Route 1.

An alternative starting point is the IGA supermarket on Route 77 in Cape Elizabeth, 4 miles south of the Million Dollar Bridge between Portland and South Portland. Starting from here shortens the ride by 2.6 miles, eliminating the section of Route 207 between Route 1 and Chamberlain Road. Directions for the ride starting from Cape Elizabeth are at the end of this tour (see page 40).

0.0 Left out of the parking lot onto Route 114.

Just ahead is Route 1, at the traffic light.

0.1 Cross Route 1 onto Route 207 (**Caution** here—this is a very busy intersection). Go 3 miles to Route 77 (Spurwink Road) on the left.

Side Trip: The loop route turns left on Route 77, but to visit Prouts Neck, continue straight for 2.6 miles until the road becomes private, and backtrack to Route 77. You'll skirt Maine's largest salt marsh on the right and Scarborough Beach on the left. The Atlantic House, a classic Victorian resort hotel, is at Scarborough Beach. At the tip of the peninsula the road hugs the ocean, passing the Black Point Inn, another elegant classic.

3.1 Turn left on Route 77 (right if you're coming from Prouts Neck) for 5.4 miles to Ocean House Road on the right. It's just after Ocean Avenue and a small snack bar on the right.

This stretch is pleasantly rural, lined with bucolic farms, well-tended fields and woodlots.

After about 3 miles, notice Sprague Hall, an old wooden grange hall, on the right at the corner of Fowler Road. Crescent Beach State Park will be on your right a mile further on.

8.5 Turn right on Ocean House Road and immediately curve left, following the main road. Go 0.7 mile to the dead end.

This is an inspiring ride along the rocky shore to Kettle Cove, a tiny beach hemmed in by outcroppings, with a grassy ribbon between the road and the beach.

9.2 From the dead end, backtrack ¼ mile to Fessenden Road, the first right.

9.5 Right for ¼ mile to the end, at the stop sign (merge right).

9.7 Bear right for 0.3 mile to a fork (the sign says "Two Lights State Park"). The route will expore both branches of the fork.

10.0 Bear right for 0.3 mile to the parking lot at the end.

The park has dramatic views from the headland worth seeing. There is a small fee for bikes. Backtrack 0.3 mile to the fork.

10.6 Take a sharp right, following the other branch of the fork, for 0.7 mile to the dead end.

There's a snack bar here, open in warm weather. You can walk out onto the rocky ledges of the small peninsula; Cape Elizabeth Light is to the left, on the other side of the cove. The second lighthouse, 300 yards west of Cape Elizabeth Light, has been restored and is privately owned.

11.3 At the dead end, make a U-turn and go 1.6 miles to the end (merge right on Route 77). There's a hill heading away from the peninsula.

12.9 Bear right for 0.3 mile to Old Ocean House Road on the right, opposite a small cemetery.

13.2 Right for 1.3 miles to a crossroads and stop sign (Route 77 again).

This is upper-crust suburbia, with gentleman farms and shorefront estates at the end of long driveways.

14.5 Right for 0.4 mile to the traffic light (Shore Road on the right).

You'll pass the Cape Elizabeth town hall, a simple wooden building, on the right. There's a snack bar in the small shopping center on the left.

14.9 Turn right on Shore Road for 2.4 miles to the entrance to Fort Williams Park on the right.

This is a pleasant ride with some views of the ocean, passing more fine houses.

17.3 Right into the park for ½ mile to Portland Head Light on the left, and backtrack to Shore Road.

Fort Williams was founded in 1873 to defend Casco Bay and remained an active military base until 1964, when it became a city park.

18.3 Right on Shore Road for 0.8 mile to Preble Steet, which bears right. The road passes seaside estates.

19.1 Bear right on Preble Street for ½ mile to the end, at the stop sign (merge right; Pillsbury Street is on the left).

There's a grocery and a snack bar at the intersection. You are now in South Portland.

19.6 Bear right (still Preble Street) for 0.3 mile to a fork where Fort Road bears right. It's a block after Beach Street, which also bears right.

19.9 Bear right on Fort Road for 0.2 mile to the crossroads and stop sign (dead end if you go straight).

Here the ride turns left, but just beyond the intersection is the Southern Maine Vocational and Technical Institute, a cluster of buildings overlooking Casco Bay. A footpath along the shore provides good views of the bay and its islands.

20.1 Left at the crossroads for less than 0.2 mile to another crossroads (Broadway) and stop sign.

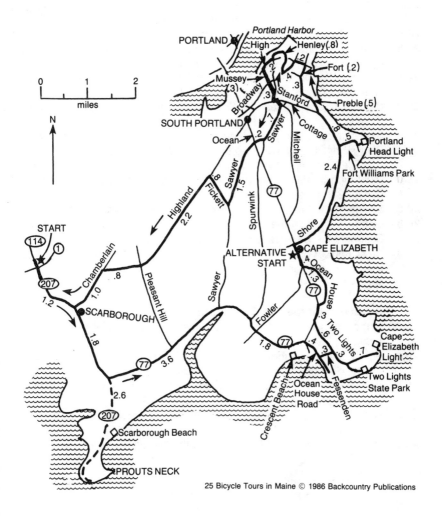

25 Bicycle Tours in Maine © 1986 Backcountry Publications

20.3   Left for 0.4 mile to Stanford Street on the right.

20.7   Turn right, and just ahead curve right on the main road (Henley Street). Continue for 0.8 mile to a crossroads (High Street) and stop sign.

> You'll go along Portland Harbor, with views of downtown Portland on the opposite shore.

21.6   Right on High Street for ¼ mile to Mussey Street, which bears left at the stop sign.

> There's a Coast Guard station on the right at the intersection.

21.8   Bear left on Mussey Street for 0.3 mile to a busy crossroads (Broadway) and stop sign.

22.1   Straight for 0.3 mile to the end (merge right opposite a cemetery).

22.4   Bear right for 1 block to the end (Cottage Road).

22.5   Left for 1 block to Mitchell Road, which bears right.

22.5   Bear right, passing the brick church on the left, for 0.1 mile to the crossroads (Sawyer Street) and a stop sign.

22.6   Turn right for 0.7 mile to the intersection where Spurwink Avenue goes straight and Sawyer Street (unmarked) turns right uphill.

23.3   Right (still Sawyer Street) for ¼ mile to the traffic light (Route 77, Ocean Avenue).

23.5   Straight for 0.4 mile to a fork where the main road bears slightly left.

23.9   Bear slightly left for 1.1 miles to the end (Fickett Street).

> The landscape thins out pleasantly.

25.0   Right (uphill) for 0.8 mile to the end. You are now in Scarborough.

25.8   Left for 2.2 miles to the crossroads (Pleasant Hill Road) and stop sign.

28.0   Straight for 0.8 mile to the end, at the stop sign (Chamberlain Road).

28.8   Left for 1 mile to the end (merge right on Route 207, Black Point Road).

29.8   Bear right for 1.2 miles to Route 1, at the traffic light.

31.0   Cross Route 1 onto Route 114 (**Caution** here). The shopping center is just ahead on your right.

Final mileage: 31.0.

Directions for the ride Cape Elizabeth start (IGA, Route 77)

0.0   Left out of parking lot for 0.2 mile to the traffic light (Shore Road is on the right).

0.2   Follow the route from mile **14.9** through the directions for mile **28.8** (merge right on Route 207, Black Point Road).

15.1   Left on Route 207 for 1.7 miles to Route 77 (Spurwink Road) on the left.

> For **Side Trip** to Prouts Neck, see mile **0.1**.

16.8   Follow the route from mile **3.1** through the directions for mile **13.2** (Route 77).

28.2   Bear right on Route 77 for 0.2 mile to the IGA on the left.

Final mileage: 28.4.

Bicycle Repair Services
Cyclemania, 59 Federal Street, Portland (774-2933)

Haggett's Cycle Shop, 34 Vannah Avenue, Portland (773-5117)
Quinn's Bike and Fitness, 140 Elm Street, Biddeford (284-4632)
Joe Jones Ski and Sport Shop, 198 Maine Mall Road, South Portland (761-1961)
Back Bay Bicycle, 33 Forest Avenue, Portland (773-6906)
Saco Cycles Unlimited, 294 Main Street, Saco (283-2453)
Allspeed Bicycle and Ski, 1041 Washington Avenue, Portland (878-8741)
Rodgers Ski and Sport, 332 Route 1, Scarborough (883-3669)

Portland Head Light, Cape Elizabeth, is Maine's first lighthouse. The tower was built in 1791.

5.

Freeport—Brunswick (or Brunswick—Freeport)

Distance: 33 miles (22 omitting South Freeport Loop, 11 omitting Brunswick Loop)

Terrain: Rolling, with several short steep hills.

Special features: L. L. Bean, Desert of Maine, harbor at South Freeport, Bowdoin College.

The area between Freeport and Brunswick is superb for bicycling, with a network of back roads winding along the Harraseeket River (a tidal inlet) and Maquoit Bay and through rich farmland just north of the coast. Thousands of motorists speed between the two communities on Interstate 95 or Route 1, unaware of the serene country roads just a couple of miles to the south.

The ride starts from Freeport, a town about 15 miles northeast of Portland. Freeport is virtually synonymous with L.L. Bean, the camping-outdoor life–sporting goods–clothing store which is the most-visited man-made attraction in Maine. In its advertisements, it bills itself as "the store that knows the outdoors"—a claim that is 100% true. No matter what you buy, you can be certain that it is practical, of good quality, fairly priced, and comes with a money-back guarantee. Stories abound of customers returning purchases several weeks or even months after purchase and receiving a refund with no questions asked. Besides functional, comfortable clothing, the store also carries an excellent selection of bicycles, cycling accessories, and bicycle clothing.

From Freeport, the route heads inland briefly to one of the state's more unusual natural attractions, the Desert of Maine. It is comprised of long strips of rippled sand, about a tenth of a mile wide, surrounded by pine trees. This desert, still growing, is the result of poor farming practices which depleted the topsoil and uncovered the sand underneath, which drifted and spread until it buried entire trees.

From the Desert of Maine, it's not far to the coast at South Freeport, a charming fishing port on the Harraseeket River, which is actually a small bay. The ride follows narrow back roads which run close to the water, passing through haystack-dotted fields that slope gently to the shore. The tour heads inland for about three miles into Brunswick, which marks the beginning of the mid-coast area. North and east of Brunswick, the coast becomes much more jagged, with a succession of peninsulas, sub-peninsulas, and countless coves and inlets until Penobscot Bay.

Brunswick (the alternative starting point) is the epitome of the gracious New England college town, and the first of the handsome coastal communities that grace Route 1 about every 10 miles until Searsport, about 75 miles up the coast. The focal point of Brunswick is Bowdoin College with its lovely campus shaded with elm trees. Bowdoin is home to two excellent museums: the Bowdoin College Museum of Art and the Peary-MacMillan Arctic Museum. Robert Peary, the first person to reach the North Pole (in 1909) was a Bowdoin graduate, as was his chief assistant, Donald MacMillan. Next to the campus stands the splendid, cross-shaped First Parish Church, which was built in 1846 in Gothic style. Downtown Brunswick, with an unusually wide main street, is just north of the college and the church. Adjacent to the downtown area are numerous fine homes from the early 19th century, including the Harriet Beecher Stowe House, where the author wrote *Uncle Tom's Cabin* between 1850 and 1852.

From Brunswick, it's about nine miles back to Freeport. Most of this section follows Pleasant Hill Road, a quiet secondary road that runs parallel to Route 1, passing through broad expanses of farmland.

Directions for the ride: Freeport start
Start from—where else?—L.L. Bean, on the north side of Route 1 in the center of town. Directions for the ride starting from Brunswick are at the end of this tour (see page 46).

The first part of the ride encompasses the western loop, which visits the Desert of Maine and South Freeport. You can shorten the ride to 22 miles by omitting this loop. If you wish to do so, start by heading east on Bow Street, which is directly opposite L.L. Bean. Go 1.5 miles to a fork where Pleasant Hill Road bears left. Pick up the tour at mile **12.0.**

0.0 Left out of the parking lot, heading east on Route 1, for 0.3 mile to Route 125 on the left (a sign says "to Interstate 95").

0.3 Left for 0.6 mile to the end (Route 125 turns right).

0.9 Left for 1.7 miles to Murch Road on the left.
        You'll pass the Pine Tree Academy, a Seventh Day Adventist school.

2.6 Left for 0.6 mile to the end (Hunter Road).

3.2 Right for 0.2 mile to the first left, Merrill Road. It comes up while you're going downhill.

3.4 Left for ½ mile to the end, at a stop sign (merge left on Desert Road).

3.9 Sharp right for 0.3 mile to the Desert of Maine at the dead end.

4.2 From the Desert of Maine, follow Desert Road for 2.2 miles to Route 1, just past the Interstate 95 interchange.
        The road goes through farmland with grazing horses and cows, up and down several short hills.

6.4   Right on Route 1 for 100 yards to Pine Street (unmarked) on the left.

6.4   Left on Pine Street for 1.4 miles to a crossroads (South Freeport Road) and
stop sign.

Caution turning left from Route 1, which is very busy. There are two
short, steep hills on Pine Street. When you get to the crossroads, there
is a grocery on the right. This is South Freeport.

7.8   Straight for 0.4 mile to the dead end, passing gracious homes.

At the end is a picturesque dock and the Harraseeket Lunch and
Lobster Company, a great spot for a snack, with excellent home-
made pies.

8.2   From the dock, backtrack 0.4 mile to South Freeport Road.

8.6   Turn right for 1.5 miles to Mast Landing Road on the right, just after a
bridge over a little inlet.

10.1 Right for 1.2 miles to the end.

At the end, the loop route turns right, but you can shorten the ride to
11 miles by turning left for 0.8 mile to the end (Route 1), opposite L.L.
Bean.

11.3 Right for 0.7 mile to a fork where Pleasant Hill Road bears left.

12.0 Bear right at the fork (a sign says "to Wolf Neck Woods State Park") for
2.1 miles to another fork where Flying Point Road curves left and Lower
Flying Point Road turns right.

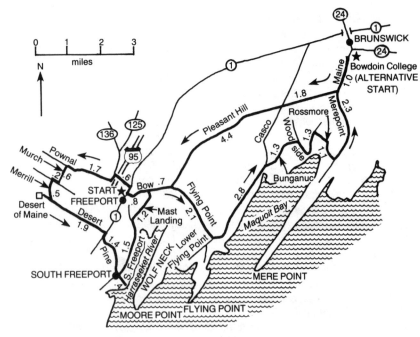

25 Bicycle Tours in Maine © 1986 Backcountry Publications

This stretch has several short, steep ups and downs.

Side Trip: After 0.8 mile, Wolf Neck Road on the right leads about 3 miles to Wolf Neck Woods State Park, a scenic preserve with hiking trails at the tip of the peninsula.

14.1 Curve left on Flying Point Road for 2.8 miles to a fork just beyond the top of a steep hill. (Bunganuc Road bears right.)

This is a lovely road, winding through broad fields with views of the bay in the distance.

16.9 Bear right at the fork for 1.3 miles to the end (Woodside Road), at the stop sign. **Caution:** This section is bumpy.

18.2 Right for 1.3 miles to Rossmore Road on the right.

Again the road passes through large fields that slope gently down to the bay.

Haystacks dot a field sloping down to Maquoit Bay, Brunswick.

19.5 Turn right on Rossmore Road for 1.1 miles to the end.

You'll pass a marker on the left indicating the site of the home of Matthew Thornton, a signer of the Declaration of Independence.

20.6 Left for 3.3 miles to Bowdoin College on the right.

The Art Museum has its own building; the Arctic Museum is in Hubbard Hall. Opposite the far end of the campus is Bowdoin Pines, a stately grove. The snack bar in Moulton Union is a good lunch spot.

23.9 From the college, backtrack 1 mile to Pleasant Hill Road, which bears right just after the hospital on the left.

24.9 Bear right for 1.8 miles to a diagonal crossroads at a "Yield" sign.

The land quickly becomes rural, with large tracts of farmland.

26.7 Straight for 4.4 miles to the end (merge right at a "Yield" sign).

This section is rolling, with several short hills. You'll pass an old, weathered cemetery on the right.

31.1 Bear right for 1.6 miles to the end (Route 1), opposite L.L. Bean.

After 0.6 mile, a small road that goes uphill is on your right. If you turn onto it, the Mast Landing Audubon Sanctuary is just ahead on the right. The 150-acre preserve has foot trails through woods and fields and along a small tidal river.

There's a tough hill about ¼ mile long just before Freeport.
Final mileage: 32.7.

Directions for the ride: Brunswick start

Start from Maine Street, which borders Bowdoin College on the west side of the campus.

0.0 Head south on Maine Street, with the college on your left, for 1 mile to Pleasant Hill Road, which bears right just after the hospital on the left.

1.0 Follow the ride from mile **24.9** to the end, opposite L.L. Bean.

At this point you can shorten the ride to 22 miles, omitting the eastern loop past the Desert of Maine and South Freeport, by backtracking on Bow Street for 1.5 miles to the fork where Pleasant Hill Road bears left, and resuming the tour at mile **12.0.**

8.7 Right on Route 1 (left if you visited L.L. Bean) for 0.3 mile to Route 125 on the left (a sign says "to Interstate 95").

9.0 Follow the tour from mile **0.3** to the college.
Final mileage: 32.7.

Bicycle Repair Services
L.L. Bean, Route 1, Freeport (865-4761)
Center Street Cycles, 11½ Center Street, Brunswick (729-5309)
National Bike Shop, Freeport (865-0523)

Mid-Coast Region

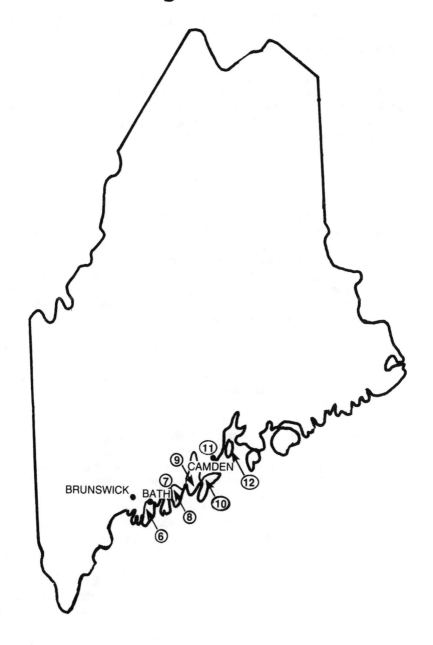

6.

Bath — Phippsburg — Popham Beach

Distance: 36 miles (16 omitting the Popham Beach Loop)
Terrain: Rolling, with several short, steep hills.
Special features: Popham Beach State Park, Fort Popham, Fort Baldwin, Maine Maritime Museum, elegant sea captains' homes in Bath.
Caution: On hot weekends, traffic on Route 209 heading to and from Popham Beach is very heavy. It's best to take this ride when it's not a beach day, or during the week.

The peninsula extending from Bath south to Small Point is the third of the nine peninsulas which characterize the mid-coast region between Brunswick and Penobscot Bay, and this peninsula is the most westerly in the book. Most of the landscape consists of low, forested hills interspersed with a few small farms. The broad tidal estuary of the Kennebec River flows along the eastern edge of the peninsula. Narrow secondary roads run parallel to Route 209, the main north-south road, enabling the cyclist to complete two short loops between Bath and Popham Beach with very little backtracking. The short ride on this tour consists of the northern loop only.

The ride starts from the western edge of Bath, a small city boasting many gracious 19th-century homes, a handsome downtown area, and the superb Maine Maritime Museum. Bath blossomed into a thriving shipbuilding center and seaport during the mid-1800s, and the well-maintained houses of successful sea captains and merchants are testimony to the city's prosperous history. Shipbuilding still dominates Bath's economy at the massive Bath Iron Works, where large naval vessels and submarines are constructed. The tall crane at the Iron Works can be seen all over the city. You'll explore Bath at the end of the ride.

From Bath, the route quickly enters rural, wooded countryside. The first few miles on secondary roads snaking down the center of the peninsula are the hilliest. After about eight miles you'll arrive at the eastern shore in the little fishing village of Phippsburg. The route now heads north, running parallel to the Kennebec River back to Bath.

The long ride continues south, looping around the southern half of the peninsula. The southern tip, Small Point, is not on the route because it is an out-and-back trip of several miles each way, with limited views of the ocean. On the southern shore you'll come to Popham Beach State Park, one of Maine's most attractive coastal areas, with a broad, sandy beach unmarred by cottages and condominiums. Just past the beach, at the eastern tip of the peninsula, are two forts, Fort Popham and Fort Baldwin. The latter, commanding the top of a hill, provides an inspiring view. Next to the forts is the small summer community of Popham Beach, where you can take advantage of a good seafood restaurant. Heading north, the route follows a narrow lane, hugging the Kennebec River, to Phippsburg, where you'll rejoin the short ride.

Directions for the ride

Start from McDonald's, Bath Shopping Center, on the north side of Route 1. If you're coming from the south on Route 1, you can't turn left into McDonald's because the highway is divided. Continue past McDonald's to the ramp leading to Route 209, which crosses above Route 1. Turn left on Route 209 and immediately turn left again on the ramp leading to Route 1 in the opposite direction. McDonald's is just ahead.

0.0   Leave the parking lot at its western end, farthest from McDonald's (don't get on Route 1). Turn left at the end of the entrance road onto Congress Avenue for 0.2 mile to the end. Congress Avenue crosses a bridge over Route 1.

0.4   Right for ¼ mile to Berrys Mill Road, which bears left.

0.6   Bear left for 3.6 miles to the end (Campbells Pond Road on the left).
        This is a lovely narrow road winding through the woods, up and down several short steep hills.

4.2   Right for 1 mile to a fork where the main road bears left.

5.2   Bear left for 1.4 miles to an unmarked road on the left at the bottom of a hill.
        This is another narrow backroad with some short ups and downs.

6.6   Left for 1.7 miles to the end (Route 209).
        This is the toughest road on the ride, with two steep hills: but hang in there! The rest of the ride is much easier. When you come to Route 209, note the fine brick house on the corner.
        Here the long ride turns right. To do the short ride, turn left on Route 209 for 4.1 miles to Webber Avenue, which bears right. There's a grocery ½ mile before the intersection, just after a small bridge. Resume at mile **32.1.** Final mileage: 16.4.

8.3   Right on Route 209 for 4.7 miles to the fork where Route 217 bears right. At the beginning of this section the road hugs the bay as it passes through the small village of Phippsburg. Notice the tiniest of post offices on your right. After ½ mile there's a grocery.

13.0 Bear left at fork (still Route 209) for 0.7 mile to the intersection where Route 209 turns left and Route 216 goes straight.

13.7 Turn left, staying on Route 209.
        After 3.3 miles, you'll pass the entrance to Popham Beach State Park on the right. Continue for 1.5 miles to the dead end. Shortly before the end is the small summer community of Popham Beach. Spinney's

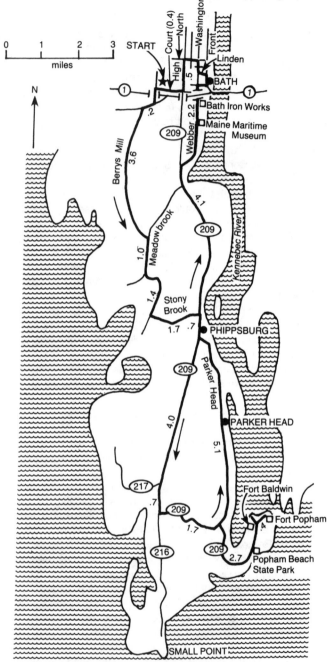

Restaurant, a reasonably priced eatery serving fresh seafood, is a great place for a halfway stop. At the end is Fort Popham, a semicircular granite fort which was begun in 1861 and never completed. It was designed to protect the mouth of the Kennebec River during the Civil War.

18.5 From Fort Popham, backtrack 0.4 mile to a narrow lane on the right. The main road curves left at the intersection.

18.9 Sharp right for 0.2 mile to the end of the paved road.

Walk your bike another few hundred yards along the series of batteries and embankments which comprise Fort Baldwin. The views are superb. At the very top of the hill is a lookout tower with the best view of all. The fort was built between 1905 and 1912 and manned during both World Wars.

This was also the site of the Popham Colony, which in 1607 was the first English colony north of Virginia. After a year the settlers became discouraged, built the first ship in the New World, and sailed back to England.

19.2 Backtrack to the main road.

19.5 Bear right on Route 209 for 2.7 miles to the point where Route 209 curves 90 degrees left and a smaller road is on the right.

22.2 Right on the smaller road for 5.1 miles to the end, where you'll merge right on Route 209.

The lovely narrow road winds along the Kennebec River, bobbing up and down small hills, to the unspoiled fishing village of Parker Head. You'll pass an old cemetery and several handsome wooden houses. At the end, notice the Phippsburg Public Library, a small wooden building built in 1923. There's also a grocery at the intersection. To your right, on Route 209, is the miniscule post office that you passed earlier.

27.3 Bear right on Route 209 for 4.8 miles to Webber Avenue, which bears right.

Hawks soared overhead while I was bicycling along this section. There'll be a grocery about ½ mile before the intersection, just after a small bridge.

32.1 Bear right on Webber Avenue for 2.2 miles to the traffic light just past the endless Bath Iron Works, a green metallic building ¼ mile long.

You'll pass the Thomas Plant Memorial Home, an elegant, white home for the elderly overlooking the river. Further along is the Percy & Small Shipyard, which is one of the three separate sites comprising the Maine Maritime Museum (you'll pass the other two sights later on the route). The shipyard has exhibits showing how the tall ships from the age of sail were constructed and an actual shop (called the Apprenticeshop) where craftsmen learn the trade of building small wooden boats. Immediately after the Iron Works, notice the fine wooden church on the left, contrasting with the industrial bleakness across the street.

At the traffic light, the road passes underneath Route 1.

34.3   Straight at the light for 1 block to a crossroads (Centre Street).

34.4   Right for 0.1 mile to the end, Front Street, at the top of the hill.

The Bath City Hall, a graceful concrete building with a cupola, stands in front of you.

34.5   Left for ¼ mile to Linden Street on the left, just past a small park.

Front Street passes through the central business district, with proud red brick buildings from the Victorian era on both sides of the street. After a long period of neglect, in the 1970s the downtown area was refurbished to its original luster.

34.7   Left on Linden Street for one block to the end (Washington Street).

Notice the yellow brick library on the left and the Gothic-style church across the street built in 1844. The church is now part of the Maine Maritime Museum and contains exhibits about ships, shipbuilders, and sailors.

34.8   Right for 0.2 mile to the second crossroads (North Street), just past the Sewell House on your right.

This building, the third site of the Maine Maritime Museum, is an impressive 30-room sea captain's mansion with period furnishings and a large collection of ship models. It was built in 1844 in grand Federal style.

Washington Street boasts the largest concentration of Bath's elegant homes. You may want to cruise slowly down to Route 1 and up to the far end of the street, admiring this showpiece of 19th-century architecture.

35.0   Left for 0.2 mile to the second crossroads (High Street), at a blinking light.

35.2   Left for ½ mile to Court Street, a crossroads on the far side of the red brick courthouse on the right.

35.7   Right on Court Street for 0.4 mile to the end. McDonald's is in front of you.

Final mileage: 36.1.

Bicycle Repair Services

Bath Cycle & Ski, Route 1, Woolwich (442-7002)

7.
Wiscasset—Head Tide—
Newcastle—Sheepscot

Distance: 32 miles
Terrain: Rolling, with several short steep hills.
Special features: Fine architecture in Wiscasset, historic villages, idyllic rolling countryside, unique country store.

Just north of Route 1, between Wiscasset and Damariscotta, is an area that is ideal for bicycling. Vacationers clog Route 27 to get to and from Boothbay Harbor or speed through on Route 1 itself, leaving the secondary roads to the north virtually untraveled. The region, though slightly inland, is still coastal in character, with tidal inlets, patches of salt marsh, and serene rolling countryside sloping to the Sheepscot and Damariscotta Rivers.

The ride starts from Wiscasset, an architectural jewel of a town about 45 miles northeast of Portland. The sign that says "Welcome to Wiscasset, prettiest village in Maine," greeting you as you enter the town from the south on Route 1, does not exaggerate. Wiscasset is highlighted by a large number of elegant mansions gracing the hillside above the Sheepscot River. Most of them were built by wealthy merchants and sea captains during the early- and middle-19th century, during Maine's heyday as a shipbuilding center and seaport. One of the more unusual mansions is the Musical Wonder House, a Greek Revival house with a collection of antique music boxes, player pianos, and other mechanical musical instruments. Two other mansions worth visiting, both built in 1807, are Castle Tucker, renowned for its graceful elliptical staircase, and the Nickels-Sortwell House, a superb Federal-style residence.

From Wiscasset, the route heads north on quiet backroads, through rolling farmland with sturdy old barns, to the historic village of Head Tide. This is a small, well-preserved 19th-century community on the National Register of Historic Places, best known as the birthplace of poet Edward Arlington Robinson in 1869.

From here, the route turns east to Damariscotta Mills, another picturesque village clinging to the steep hill above the Damariscotta River. On the way, a colorfully named country store is a good halfway stop.

You'll now head south, hugging the shore of Salt Bay, a wide tidal pool on the Damariscotta River that's a great spot to observe migrating shore birds. The route follows the bay and river to Newcastle (and its twin town of Damariscotta, just off the route), and curves west through idyllic rolling farm country to Sheepscot, another meticulously preserved 19th-century village. The final section of the ride follows the Sheepscot River back to Wiscasset, passing handsome white houses perched on the hill above the river.

Directions for the ride
Start from the Lincoln County Courthouse, Route 1, Wiscasset.

It's on the south side of Route 1, immediately east of Route 27. The courthouse is a handsome brick structure built in 1824.

0.0   Left out of the parking lot and immediately right on Route 27. Go 2 miles to an unmarked road on the right at the top of the hill (signs say "to Huntoon Hill Grange" and "to Wiscasset Speedway").

It's a steady but gentle climb out of Wiscasset.

2.0   Right for ½ mile to the end.

2.5   Right for 0.6 mile to the end.

This is a flying downhill run.

3.1   Left for 2.6 miles to an unmarked road on the right.

It's your first right, and it comes up suddenly as you start to go down a hill. You'll pass the Wiscasset Speedway, a small oval track, shortly after you turn.

5.7   Right for 1.3 miles to a crossroads (Route 218).

Here the route goes straight, but you can shorten the ride to 12 miles by turning right on Route 218 for 4.6 miles to Route 1, and right for 0.2 mile to the courthouse on the left.

7.0   Straight for 0.1 mile to the first left.

7.1   Left for 1.7 miles to the end (merge right on Route 218).

This is a lovely narrow road, ascending onto a ridge with fine views, followed by a long downhill run.

Caution: Watch for sand at the bottom of the hill.

8.8   Bear right on Route 218 for 1.4 miles to a fork (Route 218 bears left).

There's a store at the fork. Just after you merge onto Route 218, you will see a lovely little schoolhouse with a bell tower on your left, built in 1795, and a green-shuttered meetinghouse, built in 1789. This is Alna Center. Beyond, the road traverses a ridge with sweeping views. When you reach the store at the fork, look for a plaque that lists the historic buildings in the vicinity.

10.2   Bear left at the fork, staying on Route 218, for 1.3 miles to an unmarked road at the bottom of a hill.

11.5   Right for ¼ mile to Route 194, which goes both to the left and straight ahead, in Head Tide.

Just after you turn there's a small dam on the left. The pool above the dam is smothered with alewives during their spring spawning run. A path on the right leads up a short hill to a fine white church built in 1838.

11.7   Straight on Route 194 East for 3.2 miles to a small country store on the right, at an intersection. **Caution:** Watch for cracks and potholes.

> This corner has a rather earthy name, as stated on the store. This is a great halfway stop where you and your cycling companions can take pictures of each other, with the store in the background. Don't forget to buy a T-shirt.

14.9   From the store, continue on Route 194. After ½ mile you'll merge head-on into Route 215. Continue straight for 3.7 miles to the end, at a "Yield" sign at the bottom of a steep hill. Route 215 turns sharply right here.

> This is Damariscotta Mills. As you start to descend the hill into the village, notice the lovely Federal-era mansion on your left. Several smaller roads fork off the main road, but stay on Route 215.

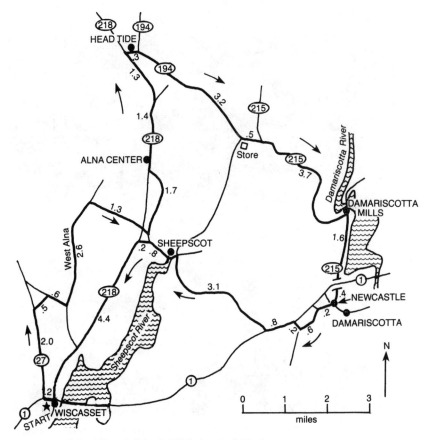

19.1   Sharp right (still Route 215) for 2 miles to a crossroads and stop sign, in the center of Newcastle.

As soon as you turn, notice the weathered church on your right. The road hugs the shore of Salt Bay, bobbing up and down little hills. After going underneath Route 1, you'll pass gracious homes and an old schoolhouse with a cupola that has been renovated into apartments.

Sheepscot: a tranquil New England village tucked away from the bustle of Route 1.

At the crossroads, Business Route 1 turns left and also goes straight ahead. The large brick church on the left on the far side of the intersection is the first Catholic church in Maine, built in 1808.

At the crossroads the ride goes straight, but if you turn left for 0.2 mile you'll come to downtown Damariscotta (see the Damariscotta-Pemaquid Point ride for more detail).

21.1 Straight at the crossroads for 0.2 mile to a smaller road that bears left as you start to go uphill.

21.3 Bear left for 0.6 mile to the fork.

The road follows the shore of the Damariscotta River.

21.9 Bear right for 0.2 mile to the end (Route 1).

22.1 Left for 0.8 mile to an unmarked road on the right that goes up a short hill (a sign may say "to Sheepscot").

22.9 Turn right. After 3.1 miles the main road turns 90 degrees left as you come into Sheepscot. Continue for 0.8 mile to a fork.

Sheepscot is a classical New England village tucked away from the bustle of Route 1. Just before the bridge over the river is a map of the historic district. There's a tough climb after the bridge.

26.8 Bear left at the fork for ¼ mile to the end (Route 218).

27.1 Left for 4.4 miles to Route 1, at the stop sign, back in Wiscasset.

About ½ mile before Route 1, you'll pass the Lincoln County Museum and Old Jail on the left. The jail, with massive granite walls more than three feet thick, was built in 1837 and used until the 1950s.

When you come to Route 1, the Nickels-Sortwell House is on your left, and a small sunken flower garden is on your right. The center of town is to your left on Route 1.

31.5 Right on Route 1 for 0.2 mile to the courthouse on the left.

If you bear left after 100 yards on High Street, the Musical Wonder House is just ahead, and Castle Tucker just beyond, opposite the end of the street.

Final mileage: 31.7.

Bicycle Repair Services
Bath Cycle & Ski, Route 1, Woolwich (442-7002)

8.

Damariscotta—Pemaquid Point—Round Pond

Distance: 40 miles
Terrain: Gently rolling, with several gradual hills and one very steep one.
Special features: Remains of fort and colonial settlement, rockbound Pemaquid Point, lighthouse, Fishermen's Museum.

The Pemaquid Peninsula, extending from Damariscotta and Waldoboro south to Pemaquid Point, is the sixth of the nine fingers of land between Brunswick and Penobscot Bay. It's an enjoyable place for bicycling, with primarily gently rolling terrain and moderate traffic. Most tourists either don't get beyond Boothbay Harbor, on the next peninsula to the west, or they bypass the Pemaquid region by zipping along Route 1 toward Bar Harbor.

The ride starts from Damariscotta, an attractive town at the head of the Damariscotta River, which is a long tidal inlet. In the center of town, handsome brick mercantile buildings from the late-19th century line both sides of the main street, which slopes upward to a graceful white church. In town is the Chapman-Hall House, a pre-Revolutionary dwelling built in 1753, with furnishings from the Colonial era and an herb garden.

From Damariscotta, the route follows the river along the western shore of the peninsula to Pemaquid Point, at the bottom. You'll have nice views of the river and some of the small coves that branch off of it. On a small promontory about three miles north of the bottom are two adjacent historic sites, Fort William Henry and Colonial Pemaquid.

Fort William Henry, a round granite building, was built in 1692. It claimed to be the largest and strongest fort in North America, but was destroyed by the French four years later. The present structure is a replica.

Colonial Pemaquid is a collection of cellar holes from a small settlement going back to the early 1600s, including several dwellings, the town hall, a tavern, forge, and stockade. It's surprising how small the houses were—only about 10 feet on each side. The other buildings aren't much bigger. Next to the cellar holes is a museum displaying a large collection of artifacts dug up from the site. If you're an archaeology buff, leave time to explore and enjoy yourself. For those less enthusiastic about artifacts, just south of the historic sites is sandy Pemaquid Beach.

Pemaquid Point is a splendid example of the tried-and-true phrase "rockbound coast of Maine." The surf crashes against windswept ledges of flat rocks, while pointed firs stand sentinel on the shore. Perched next to the rocks is the small, simple Pemaquid Point Light, built in 1824. It is connected to a white house which was originally the quarters of the lighthouse keeper and is now a museum of the fishing industry. Standing behind the lighthouse, on a clear day you can see Monhegan Island, 15 miles out to sea.

From Pemaquid Point, the route follows the eastern shore of the peninsula before cutting west back to Damariscotta. Two miles north of the point is the charming village of New Harbor, fronting on a small inlet smothered with lobster boats and sailing craft and docks piled high with neatly stacked lobster traps. About seven miles up the coast is the unspoiled lobster port of Round Pond.

Directions for the ride

Start from the municipal parking lot on Business Route 1 in the center of Damariscotta. It's on the south side of the road behind the brick business buildings, immediately east of the bridge connecting Damariscotta and Newcastle.

0.0   Right out of the parking lot for 0.1 mile to Route 129 South, which bears right at the church at the top of the hill.

0.1   Bear right for 3 miles to the fork where Route 129 bears right and Route 130 bears left.

The road follows a ridge with views of the bay down below. It's a pleasant ride.

3.1   Bear right on Route 129 for 3.4 miles to an unmarked road on the right, shortly after a small church on the right.

Notice the apple orchard on the far corner. The road goes up and down some gentle hills, through a mixture of woods and farmland.

6.5   Right on the unmarked road for 2.8 miles to a crossroads (Route 129).

The road dips down to a cove, and then climbs steeply up the toughest hill of the ride. You will come to the crossroads while going down a steep hill.

Side Trip (14 miles): At the crossroads the loop route goes straight, but if you turn right on Route 129 you'll come to South Bristol and Christmas Cove, picturesque fishing and yachting villages at the tip of a smaller peninsula just west of the main one. After 5 miles you'll come to South Bristol, where the road crosses a small drawbridge. At the top of the tough hill after the bridge, turn right on West Side Road for 1.4 miles, following the shore of Rutherford Island, to the end (Route 129 again). Turn right for 1 mile to the dead end, going through Christmas Cove. At the point where the road forks into private dead-end roads, turn around and follow Route 129 for about 6.5 miles back to the loop route.

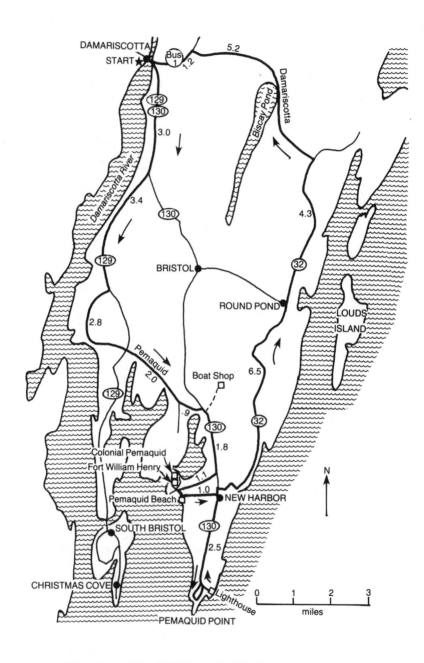

9.3 Straight at the crossroads (right if you visited Christmas Cove) for 2 miles to a fork where the main road curves left.

You'll pass the Harrington Meeting House, a simple church built in 1772, containing exhibits of local history.

11.3 Curve left at the fork for 0.9 mile to the end (Route 130).

There's an old-fashioned country store on the right just before the end.

12.2 Turn right on Route 130 for 1.8 miles to an unmarked road on the right, at a traffic island (a sign says "to Colonial Pemaquid").

There's a gas station on the right just before the intersection. If you take your first left off Route 130 (after 0.2 mile) and go about a mile to the end of the paved road, you'll come to Carpenter's Boat Shop, where apprentices learn the craft of building small wooden boats.

The sea crashes against rocky ledges near New Harbor.

14.0 Right on the unmarked road for 1.1 miles to a crossroads.

Here the ride turns left, but to visit Fort William Henry and Colonial Pemaquid, turn right and immediately right again on the gravel road. The fort is just ahead on the left, and Colonial Pemaquid is 0.3 mile beyond the fort.

15.1 Left at the crossroads (straight if you visited the historic sites) for 1 mile to the end, Route 130, in New Harbor.

Pemaquid Beach, the only sand beach on the peninsula, is on your right just beyond the crossroads, set back from the road.

16.1 Right on Route 130 for 2.5 miles to a fork where Route 130 curves sharply left and a smaller road bears right.

There's a sign for the Bradley Inn at the intersection.

18.6 Bear right for 0.9 mile to the end (Route 130 again).

This is a lovely narrow road hugging the rocky coast at the extreme southern tip of the peninsula. You'll pass gracious homes and estates and get a view of Pemaquid Point Light across a small cove. At the end, the Hotel Pemaquid, an ornate Victorian classic, stands in front of you.

19.5 Right for 0.1 mile to the dead end, at the lighthouse and Fishermen's Museum.

Spend some time exploring the ledges. The dark rocks are striped with narrow, light-colored bands.

19.6 From the lighthouse, follow Route 130 for 2.9 miles to Route 32 on the right.

Just before the intersection is the center of the lovely village of New Harbor, set back from the road on the right. An elegant cedar-shingled church fronts on the small green. There is also a grocery and snack bar.

22.5 Right on Route 32 for 6.5 miles to the village of Round Pond.

Shortly after you turn onto Route 32, the road hugs the shore of New Harbor, a small inlet crammed with lobster craft, sailboats, and perhaps a tall-masted schooner.

Round Pond is an attractive lobster port with a grocery, big white houses, and a traditional New England church.

29.0 Continue on Route 32 for 4.3 miles to an unmarked road on the left that climbs a short hill (a sign says "to Damariscotta").

33.3 Left for 5.2 miles to the end (Business Route 1).

This is a smooth secondary road bobbing up and over short wooded hills. Halfway along you'll pass Biscay Pond on the left. The small beach here is a good spot for a swim before the end of the ride.

38.5 Left on Business Route 1 for 1.2 miles to the parking lot on the left.

Final mileage: 39.7.

9.

Wyeth Country: Waldoboro— Friendship—Cushing—Warren—Union

Distance: 29 miles (48 with Warren-Union extension)
Terrain: Rolling, with several short, steep hills.
Special features: Unspoiled old towns, bay views, beautiful rolling farmland.

Here is a tour of two distinct regions: the peninsula pointing south between Waldoboro and Thomaston, and, on the long ride, the rolling, lake-dotted farming country north of those two towns. Both regions possess the quiet charm of antique towns which are not commonly visited and the serenity of pastures of grazing horses and cows, silhouetted by tottering barns and old farmhouses. With the exception of Route 1, the roads in the region are lightly traveled, because nearly all tourists heading up the coast take Route 90 between Route 1 and Camden, or they stay on Route 1 to Thomaston without venturing south.

The short ride starts from Waldoboro and follows the western shore of the peninsula to Friendship, on one of the three subpeninsulas that form its southern edge. The Friendship peninsula is the eighth and the chubbiest of the nine closely-spaced promontories between Brunswick and Penobscot Bay. Its landscape is common to most of the mid-coast region's peninsulas, with continuous short rolling hills and open ridges with views of the bay in the distance.

Waldoboro is a marvelous Victorian town that clings to the steep hillside rising from the east bank of the Medomak River. It is virtually unvisited because it is bypassed by Route 1 a mile to the north. A short row of 19th-century brick buildings forms the business district. Friendship is an equally sleepy village with some gracious homes rimming the tip of the peninsula and a small harbor bobbing with sailing craft, lobster boats, and perhaps a couple of Friendship sloops. The latter, first built in the town in the 1870s, are renowned for their seaworthiness, speed, and grace. The town hosts an annual Friendship Day Festival in late July when owners of the sloops sail them in the harbor. From Friendship, the ride heads up the middle of the peninsula, along a ridge with fine views, and returns to Waldoboro on Route 1.

The long ride follows the eastern shore of the peninsula, bordered by the broad St. George River, to Cushing and Thomaston. Cushing is a tiny hamlet with a general store and a few fishermen's houses surrounded by large fields undulating across the landscape. The community is best known as the locale of many of Andrew Wyeth's paintings, including his well-known work "Christina's World," which portrays a woman lying on a broad, sloping field with a lonely house on the horizon.

The ride skirts Thomaston, at the northeast corner of the peninsula, and heads inland to Warren, another completely unspoiled Victorian town that clings to both sides of a steep, narrow valley. The countryside heading north to Union and back to Waldoboro is idyllic, with prosperous rolling farmland bordered by wooded hills and views of the distant Camden Hills across Seven Tree Pond.

Union is yet another museum-piece New England town perched on a hillside, built around a large, sloping green with a bandstand on one side and a monument on the other.

Directions for the 48-mile ride

Start from Moody's Diner at the junction of Routes 1 and 220 in Waldoboro. The parking lot across from the restaurant is out of harm's way. Moody's is a classic wooden 1930s diner that has been a Route 1 landmark for over 50 years. It's a great place to eat before and after the ride, and it's very reasonably priced.

0.0   Head south on Route 220, passing Moody's on the left, for 0.6 mile to the crossroads where Route 220 turns left, midway down the steep hill (**Caution:** The descent is very steep, and the intersection comes up suddenly.)

Just after you begin, you'll pass the Waldoboro Historical Society Museum on the right. It contains a cluster of buildings, including an old barn, a one-room schoolhouse built in 1857, a cattle pound, and a turn-of-the-century farm kitchen. As you start down the long hill, notice the fine white church on the left. Just before the crossroads is the small, yellow-brick library.

0.6   Left at the crossroads (still Route 220) for 9.4 miles to the end (Route 97), in Friendship, at the top of the steep hill.

As soon as you turn you'll pass the old business district of Waldoboro. Just ahead, behind the church on the right, notice the wooden Victorian factory with a cupola. As you head toward Friendship, the road ascends onto a ridge with fine views of the bay in the distance.

After 9 miles, at the point where a side road bears to the right, there's a one-room brick schoolhouse, also built in 1857, that is now the Friendship Museum. It contains early local artifacts, marine exhibits, and material on the Friendship sloop.

Side Trip: The side road leads 2.6 miles to the tip of Martin Point. The road hugs the shore of Hatchet Cove, passing docks stacked with lobster traps, pine groves, and gracious homes nestled in the pines at the end of the peninsula.

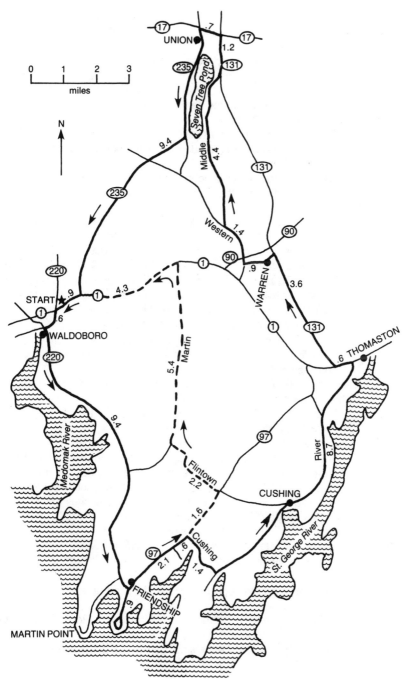

10.0   Right at the end of Route 220 for 0.9 mile to a fork where a smaller road bears right.

10.9   Bear right on the smaller road. After 0.6 mile the main road curves left up-hill. Continue for 0.9 mile to the stop sign. You're back in Friendship.

You'll pass handsome shingled houses along the rim of the small peninsula just south of the center of town.

12.4   Straight onto Route 97 for 2.1 miles to an unmarked road on the right. Continue straight for 0.6 mile to the next right, an unmarked road that goes downhill. Telephone pole number 86 (the bottom number) is on the left opposite the intersection.

(Here the long ride turns right and the short ride goes straight.) Just past the stop sign is the center of Friendship and a small grocery.

15.1   Right for 1.4 miles to the end.

The road dips down to an inlet and then climbs a short, steep hill.

16.5   Left for 8.7 miles to the end (Route 1), on the outskirts of Thomaston.

After three miles you'll pass the country store in Cushing. Beyond, the road winds through large farms with the St. George River in the distance. To your left you can see the State Prison. You'll pass a snack bar about a mile before Route 1. Just ahead, you'll descend steeply to a bridge. Curve left on the main road immediately after the bridge.

25.2   Left on Route 1 for 0.6 mile to Route 131, which bears right.

The prison is on your left as soon as you turn. (Thomaston, which has many fine houses, is to your right on Route 1. For more detail, see the Thomaston Ride.)

25.8   Bear right on Route 131 for 3.6 miles to a road on the left that is 100 yards before a sign that says "Junction, Route 90."

If you come to Route 90 you've gone 0.2 mile too far. The road is immediately after a garage on the left.

29.4   Left for 0.9 mile to a fork with a monument in the middle.

The road drops very steeply into Warren. Immediately after the bridge is a grocery on the right. Across from it is an old wooden mill. As you start to climb the short, steep hill out of Warren, notice the fine field-stone library on the right and the two white churches further on.

30.3   Straight at fork (don't bear left) for 50 feet to the end, and right for 0.1 mile to the crossroads (Route 90) and stop sign.

30.4   Straight for 1.4 miles to the second right, Middle Road.

31.8   Right for 4.4 miles to the end, at the top of the hill (merge left on Route 131).

The road winds through rich farmland, rolling up and down several short steep hills.

36.2   Bear left on Route 131 for 1.2 miles to the crossroads (Route 17) and stop sign.

At the beginning, notice the small dam with a gorge at the bottom on the left.

37.4   Left on Route 17 for 0.7 mile to a crossroads (Route 235 on the left).
Elmer's Restaurant, a good lunch spot, is on the far side of the intersection. **Caution:** Route 17 is a busy road with no shoulder. Keep to the right.

38.1   Left on Route 235 for 9.4 miles to the end (Route 1).
After ¼ mile you'll come to the Union town green. **Caution:** At the green, a crossroads and stop sign come up suddenly while you're going downhill. Notice the large, wooden Masonic Temple on your left. On the right, a map on the green shows the town as it existed during the early 1800s. Beyond Union, the road follows Seven Tree Pond, with views of the Camden Hills across the water. The best views are back over your left shoulder.

47.5   Right on Route 1 for 0.9 mile to the parking lot on the right.
Final mileage: 48.4.

Directions for the 29-mile ride

0.0   Follow the long ride through the directions for mile **12.4.**

15.1   Continue straight on Route 97 for 1.6 miles to a road on the left that is immediately before a road on the right. A sign at the intersection says "to Warren (straight) and to Cushing (right)."

16.7   Left for 2.2 miles to the end.

18.9   Right for 5.4 miles to the end (Route 1).
You'll climb gradually onto a ridge with a sweeping view. **Caution:** After about 5 miles, slow down for railroad tracks while you're going downhill.

24.3   Left on Route 1 for 4.3 miles to the parking lot on the right.
Caution: There is no shoulder on Route 1 for the first 1.2 miles. Keep to the right. The rest of Route 1 has a wide shoulder.
Final mileage: 28.6.

Bicycle Repair Services
Maine Sport, 24 Main Street, Camden (236-8797)
Oggibike, 29 Mountain Street, Camden (236-3631)

10.

Lighthouses and Lobsters: Thomaston— Port Clyde—Owls Head

Distance: 50 miles with Port Clyde loop; shorter loop: 30 miles
Terrain: Gently rolling, with a few moderate hills. This is one of the easier peninsular rides.
Special features: Historic mansion, Owls Head Transportation Museum, lighthouses.

The peninsula extending from Thomaston and Rockland south to Port Clyde is the most easterly of the nine closely spaced fingers of land jabbing the coast between Brunswick and Penobscot Bay. North of Rockland the coastline suddenly smooths out along the bay's western shore. Traffic on this ride is refreshingly light—much of it doesn't get beyond Boothbay Harbor, and most northbound travelers bypass Thomaston by shortcutting to Camden on Route 90.

The ride starts from Thomaston, a gracious coastal town. In the center of town are a graceful white church and a compact business block of three-story brick buildings, built during the turn of the century, which face each other across Route 1. Elegant wooden Federal-era and Victorian houses, originally built by sea captains, grace Route 1 on both sides of downtown. The most impressive house is Montpelier, a replica of the mansion built in 1794 for Henry Knox, the nation's first Secretary of War. The Federal-style residence boasts a bowed front and a large, glassed-in widow's walk. In contrast, the Maine State Prison, at the west end of town, seems out of place.

From Thomaston, the route heads south along the St. George River, passing large farms with views of the water in the distance. Just beyond the tiny community of St. George, the ride cuts east across the peninsula and then northeast along the opposite shore to the fishing village of Owls Head. A back road leads to Owls Head Light at the eastern tip, a spectacular spot with high, sheer cliffs rimmed by pines.

A worthwhile side trip, a little over a mile off the route, is a visit to the Owls Head Transportation Museum, which has a collection of antique cars and airplanes. A unique feature of the museum is that many of the exhibits are kept in working order, with demonstrations given on weekends.

The longer ride continues south from St. George to Port Clyde, at the southern tip of the peninsula. Port Clyde is a classic Maine village, with rickety wharves perched on pilings, a small harbor filled with lobster boats, and stacks of lobster traps everwhere. The ferry to Monhegan Island, 11 miles out to sea, leaves from here. At the extreme tip is Marshall Point Light, a small white lighthouse next to a gambrel-roofed keeper's residence (the lighthouse is now automated).

From Port Clyde, the road winds north along the opposite shore of the peninsula to Tenants Harbor, another attractive lobster port. Smaller than Port Clyde, the compact village contains a simple white church, an old wooden schoolhouse, and a cluster of neat wooden houses with peaked roofs. The route continues north to St. George, where it rejoins the shorter ride.

Directions for the 50-mile ride

Start at the municipal parking lot in the center of Thomaston, behind the business block on the north side of Route 1.

0.0 Left (east) on Route 1 for 0.6 mile to Route 131 on the right.
Montpelier is on the far side of the intersection.

0.6 Right on Route 131 for 5.5 miles to Route 73 on the left. (Here the short ride turns left.) There are good views of the bay across fields.

6.1 Straight on Route 131 for 1.5 miles to a smaller road that bears right.

7.6 Bear right for 2.5 miles to the end (merge left at the stop sign).
This is a lovely narrow road with views of the bay.

0.1 Sharp right for 2.2 miles to the first right, just after a small cove.

2.3 Right for 2.3 miles to the crossroads (Route 131), and stop sign in Port Clyde.

4.6 Right for 0.3 mile to the dead end.
Just before the end are the Monhegan ferry terminal, an old general store, and a coffee shop.

4.9 Backtrack 0.1 mile to the first right, at the top of the steep hill.

5.0 Right for 0.4 mile to the end.

5.4 Right for 0.6 mile to the dead end.
The road hugs the rocky coast to Marshall Point Light.

6.0 At the lighthouse, make a U-turn and go 0.9 mile to the end of this road.

6.9 Right for 1 mile to the end (Route 131).

7.9 Right for 7.8 miles to Route 73 on the right.
The road passes through Tenants Harbor, where there's a grocery.

5.7 Right for 3.5 miles to the point where Route 73 curves 90 degrees left and a smaller road goes straight.
Side Trip: Here the loop route turns left, but if you go straight for 1.5 miles you'll come to Spruce Head Island. It's a lovely ride, hugging the coast, passing docks and weathered lobster sheds. Just before the end, bear right at the fork and ride along the water. At the end of the paved road you'll see tiny Burnt Island, linked to Spruce Head by a private wooden bridge.

9.2 Left on Route 73 (right if you're coming from Spruce Head) for 0.6 mile to Waterman Beach Road on the right, at the top of a short hill.

29.8 Right for 1.9 miles to the end (Route 73).

The narrow lane winds through a pastoral landscape of old barns and pastures of grazing cows and horses.

31.7 Right for 1.8 miles to the point where Route 73 turns left and a smaller road goes straight.

There is a grocery on the corner. This is the village of South Thomaston.

33.5 Straight on the smaller road for 2.2 miles to the end (Ash Point Drive).

35.7 Left for 0.4 mile to South Shore Drive on the right.

36.1 Right for 1.1 miles to Crescent Beach Road on the right, as you start to climb a short hill.

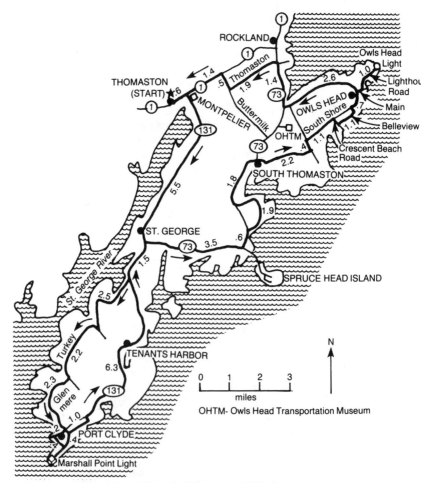

OHTM- Owls Head Transportation Museum

25 Bicycle Tours in Maine © 1986 Backcountry Publications

37.2 Right for 0.2 mile to the first left, Belleview Street.

37.4 Left for 1.1 miles to the end (South Shore Drive again).

You will pass gracious shingled homes overlooking the ocean.

38.5 Right for 0.7 mile to Main Street, which bears right at a grassy traffic island.

39.2 Bear right for 0.2 mile to Lighthouse Road on the left.

Here the ride turns left, but if you go straight for 0.1 mile you'll come to the Owls Head dock.

39.4 Left on Lighthouse Road. After 0.6 mile, the road turns to dirt. Go 0.2 mile to fork. Continue straight (don't bear left) for 0.2 mile to Owls Head Light.

40.4 From the lighthouse, backtrack 1 mile to Main Street.

41.4 Right for 0.2 mile to the end, South Shore Drive.

41.6 Right for 2.6 miles to Route 73.

Side Trip: Here the ride turns right, but to go to the Transportation Museum, turn left on Route 73 for 0.8 mile to the entrance road on the left. The museum is ½ mile down this road.

44.2 Right on Route 73 for 1.4 miles to a crossroads. Crescent Street is on the right, and Thomaston Street is on the left.

There is a grocery on the left after 1 mile.

45.6 Left at the crossroads for 1.9 miles to the end.

The large building in the distance on your right is a cement plant. You'll pass it later on the route.

47.5 Right for ½ mile to the end (Route 1).

48.0 Left for 2 miles to the center of Thomaston.

The parking lot is behind the business block on the right.

Final mileage: 50.0.

Directions for the 30-mile ride

0.0 Follow the first two directions of the long ride, to the point where Route 73 turns left off Route 131.

6.1 Left on Route 73 for 3.5 miles to the point where Route 73 curves 90 degrees left and a smaller road goes straight.

For the **Side Trip** to Spruce Head Island, see mile **25.7** of long ride.

9.6 Follow directions to the long ride from mile **29.2** to the end of the tour.

Final mileage: 30.4.

Bicycle Repair Services

Maine Sport, 24 Main Street, Camden (236-8797)

Oggibike, 29 Mountain Street, Camden (236-3631)

11.

Rockport—Camden

Distance: 25 miles
Terrain: Gently rolling, with several short, steep hills and two long, steady ones.
Special features: Picturesque harbors at Rockport and Camden, windjammer fleet, craft shops, Megunticook Lake, side trip to Mount Battie.

The Camden area, on the western shore of Penobscot Bay, about halfway between Portland and Acadia National Park, has a special appeal. Small harbors with sleek yachts and tall-masted sailing craft are framed by the wooded Camden Hills, which rise abruptly just behind the shore. Craft shops and galleries in 19th-century mercantile buildings line the streets fronting on the harbor. A few miles inland is Megunticook Lake, with its shoreline convoluted by an infinity of little coves and promontories, surrounded by green hills and meadows sloping to the water's edge.

The ride starts from Rockport, a quiet coastal town that is two miles south of Camden, its livelier and better-known neighbor. Tourists making the pilgrimage along Route 1 have to seek Rockport out or know about it in advance, because one must leave the highway onto an unmarked side street to get to the town. Rockport's small, teardrop-shaped harbor is a gem, with a waterfront park and a boatbuilding school called the Apprenticeshop (open to visitors) on the western shore.

From Rockport, you'll follow small roads that hug the shore of Penobscot Bay to Camden, a pearl on the necklace of the mid-coast towns along Route 1. In contrast to Rockport, Camden is packed with visitors to the well-stocked craft shops, galleries and restaurants lining the harbor. Camden's main street is Route 1 itself, which means that nearly every vacationer heading up the coast stops in town. With its backdrop of rugged hills, Camden Harbor is unusually picturesque. Most of Maine's windjammers, the graceful schooners that take vacationers on week-long cruises up and down the coast, are based here. Camden is also host to one of Maine's fine summer theaters, the Camden Shakespeare Company.

Although crowded, Camden is compact. The route heads inland away from the town on a secondary road, and within a half mile the traffic suddenly disappears. After about three miles, you'll come to Megunticook Lake and follow its shore, passing cozy waterfront cottages nestled in the pines. At the northern tip of the ride is the tiny village of Lincolnville Center, which consists of a few rambling old farmhouses and an old-fashioned country store. The route now turns south, paralleling the opposite shore of the lake back to Camden. Here you'll pick up a side road back to Rockport that runs along a hillside with views of the bay in the distance.

Directions for the ride

Start from the Rockport Baptist Church on Pascal Avenue, 0.2 mile east of Route 1. Park on Pascal Avenue. If you're coming from the south or west, approach Rockport on Route 90. Cross Route 1 and go 0.2 mile to the end (Pascal Avenue). Turn left, and the church is just ahead. If you're coming from the north, follow Route 1 to Route 90 on the right, at a crossroads, 2 miles south of Camden. Turn left for 0.2 mile to the end (Pascal Avenue). Turn left, and the church is just ahead.

0.0 Head north on Pascal Avenue, with the church on the left and Rockport Harbor on the right, for 0.2 mile to the end, on the far side of the bridge.

From the bridge, there's a good view of the boat-filled harbor on the right.

0.2 Right on the far side of the bridge for 0.2 mile to the intersection at the top of the hill where the main road bears right and another road turns left (a sign for the road on the left says "to Camden"). You'll go through the center of Rockport.

0.4 Bear right (this is Russell Street) for 1 mile to Bayview Street on the right.

If you wish, you can take a more scenic route which has a mile of dirt road and is 2 miles longer. It follows the harbor to Deadman Point and then curves north along the bay, passing the idyllic Vesper Hill Chapel and its lovely gardens. For the alternative route, turn right after 1 block onto Mechanic Street. After 0.4 mile the road becomes dirt. **Caution:** The dirt section has some steep pitches where the surface is loose; it's safest to walk your bike. The dirt stretch lasts about a mile; then the road curves sharply left and becomes paved again. Continue 0.9 mile to the end. Shortly after the pavement resumes, the Vesper Hill Chapel is on your left, on the brow of a bluff above the bay. At the end, turn right for 0.6 mile to Bayview Street on the right.

1.4 Right on Bayview Street for 1.7 miles to the end, in Camden (merge right on Route 1).

Craft shops, galleries, and antique shops line the road at the end. The harbor behind the shops usually has a few windjammers at anchor.

3.1 Bear right on Route 1 for 0.1 mile to the first right.

Notice the handsome red brick library on the far corner.

3.2 Right for 0.2 mile to the end.

You'll pass the Bok Amphitheatre, a lovely terraced area overlooking the harbor, where concerts and productions of the Camden Shakespeare Company are held, on the left.

3.4   Left for 0.1 mile to the crossroads (Route 1).

Side Trip: The loop route turns left on Route 1, but if you'd like to climb Mount Battie, turn right on Route 1 for 1.4 miles to the entrance to Camden Hills State Park on the left. You'll pass Norumbega on the right, an ornate mansion, now an inn, that looks like a castle. Turn left into the park. Just past the entrance booth, turn left for 1.5 miles to the top. The climb is quite steep. At the top, the stone observation tower provides an unparalleled view of Camden, the bay and its islands, and Megunticook Lake.

3.5   Left on Route 1 (straight if you're coming from Mount Battie) for 0.2 mile to Route 52 (Mountain Street) on the right.

Camden Harbor, framed by rugged hills, is unusually picturesque.

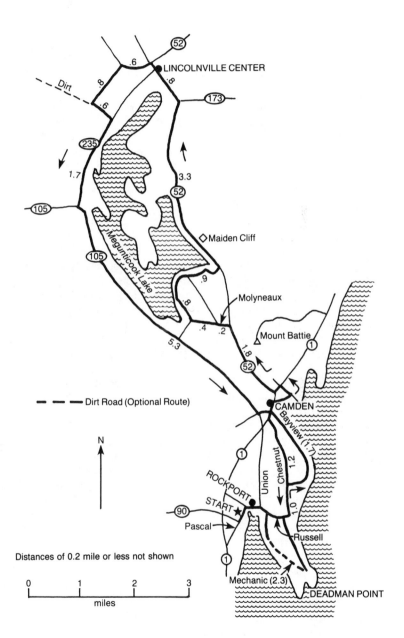

LINCOLNVILLE CENTER

52

.6

.8

Dirt

.6

235

173

1.7

3.3

105

52

◇ Maiden Cliff

105

Megunticook Lake

.9

Molyneaux

.8

.4 .2

Mount Battie △

1

5.3

1.8

52

— — — Dirt Road (Optional Route)

N

CAMDEN

Bayview (1.1)

1

Chestnut

Union

1.2

ROCKPORT

START ★

90

1.0

Pascal

Russell

Distances of 0.2 mile or less not shown

1

0   1   2   3

Mechanic (2.3)

DEADMAN POINT

miles

25 Bicycle Tours in Maine © 1986 Backcountry Publications

3.7   Right for 1.8 miles to Molyneaux Road on the left, at a traffic island.
          There's a long, gradual climb to get out of Camden and a good view
          of the Camden Hills on the right just before the intersection.
5.5   Turn left on Molyneaux Road. After ¼ mile a road bears right, but con-
          tinue straight for 0.4 mile to a fork.
6.2   Bear right at the fork. After 0.8 mile a road bears right, but continue
          straight for 0.9 mile to the end (Route 52).
          This is a delightful wooded road hugging Megunticook Lake. On the
          hillside on the opposite shore is Maiden Cliff, a dramatic 800-foot
          plunge.
7.9   Left on Route 52 for 1.8 miles to a fork where Route 52 curves left.
          The road follows the lake closely, passing beneath Maiden Cliff.
9.7   Curve left for 1.5 miles to another fork (Route 52 curves left again).
11.2 Curve left (still Route 52) for 0.8 mile to the crossroads where Route 52
          turns right, in Lincolnville Center.
          The country store on the right just before the intersection is a good
          halfway stop.
12.0 Left at the crossroads for 0.6 mile to a fork.
12.6 Bear left. After 0.8 mile, the main road curves 90 degrees left at the bottom
          of the hill. Continue for 0.6 mile to the end (Route 235).
          There's a tough hill after the fork. At the top, the wooded hill in front of
          you is Hatchet Mountain. After the road curves left, you'll have
          dramatic views of the Camden Hills.
14.0 Right on Route 235 for 1.7 miles to the end (Route 105).
15.7 Left for 5.3 miles to the crossroads (a sign says "Do not enter" if you go
          straight).
          You're back in Camden. This section has a few moderate hills. At the
          end, a millstream flows beneath the buildings on both sides of the
          road.
21.0 Left at the crossroads for 0.1 mile to another crossroads (Route 1).
21.1 Jog right on Route 1 and immediately left on Chestnut Street for 2.2 miles
          to a fork and stop sign, in Rockport.
          Just after you turn left on Chestnut Street, notice the classic white
          church on the right, and then a handsome stone one just ahead.
          Caution: Be careful making the left turn onto Chestnut Street.
          This street has diagonal parking, so watch for cars backing up.
23.3 Bear left downhill at the fork for 0.2 mile to Pascal Avenue on the left, at the
          bottom of the hill.
23.5 Left across the bridge for 0.2 mile to the starting point.
          Final mileage: 24.7.

Bicycle Repair Services

Maine Sport, 24 Main Street, Camden (236-8797)
Maine Sport, Route 1, Rockport (236-8799)
Oggibike, 29 Mountain Street, Camden (236-3631)

12.

Islesboro

Distance: 28 miles
Terrain: Rolling, with two short, steep hills and two long, steady ones.
Special features: Bay views, fine summer homes, fishing village.

Of the dozens of islands which dot the Maine coast, Islesboro is by far the finest for bicycling. It has everything that you would hope to see on a Maine island—small roads winding along the shore, stately summer homes perched on hills above the bay, coves with lobster boats and spindly piers, and peaceful villages with trim white houses. Traffic on the island is very light because the ferry can carry only about 30 cars. Islesboro is also easy to get to—it's only a 20-minute ride on the ferry, and there are several boats a day during the warmer half of the year.

Islesboro is a stringbean-shaped island, about 10 miles long, in the middle of Penobscot Bay. The island lies about two miles from the bay's western shore and three miles from its eastern shore. The ride starts from the ferry dock on the island's western side and heads to the southern tip, Pendleton Point. After five miles, you'll arrive in the wealthy summer enclave of Dark Harbor, one of the two communities on the island. The center of town contains a few modest buildings, in contrast with the large, gracious houses along the shore as you come into and then leave the village. South of Dark Harbor, the road follows a ridge with views of the bay and summer estates on both sides.

North of Dark Harbor, the character of the island changes. The summer estates give way to modest, well-kept houses where lobstermen, carpenters, and other year-round residents live. Three and a half miles north of Dark Harbor is Islesboro, the island's other community, fronting on a small bay. The rest of the ride loops around the northern half of the island, which is thinly populated. The road climbs onto gradual hills, with views of the bay in the distance. You'll pass the Islesboro Historical Society Museum, a fascinating place to visit. The last three miles hug the coast, with dramatic views of the Camden Hills across the bay.

Directions for the ride
The ferry leaves from Lincolnville, which is 5.5 miles north of Camden.

0.0 From the ferry dock on the island, head away from the dock for 1.1 miles to the end.

1.1   Right, following the sign for Dark Harbor, for 1.2 miles to the end.
This road is mostly wooded.

2.3   Right for 1 mile to the first right.

3.3   Right for 1.6 miles to the end, in Dark Harbor.
The narrow road passes shorefront estates, with views of the Camden Hills on the other side of the bay. After 1 mile, a dirt road on the right (at a crossroads) leads for 0.3 mile onto a small point lined with elegant summer residences. Just before the end, the Blue Heron Restaurant on the left is a good spot for lunch.

4.9   Turn right at the end. After 2.1 miles the road becomes dirt. Continue for 0.2 mile to the dead end, at Pendleton Point.
As soon as you turn right, the pool-like harbor, with only a narrow opening to the bay, is on your left. Just ahead are two short, steep hills. As you're climbing the second hill, notice the handsome brown church, with a belfry, on the right. At Pendleton Point there's a little beach tucked between rocky, spruce-rimmed headlands.

7.2   From Pendleton Point, follow the main road for 5.9 miles to a fork (the sign says "to the ferry," if you bear left, and "to Pripet," if you bear right).
Shortly before the fork is the village of Islesboro, with a few houses, a simple church, and a graceful fieldstone library with a small portico.

A gentleman farm in Islesboro.

Just after the library, a side road on the right hugs the harbor for 0.6 mile to a dead end.

13.1 Bear right at the fork for 2.7 miles to another fork.

You'll immediately pass the Historical Society Museum and a Masonic hall on your left, both traditional white buildings with peaked roofs. Beyond is a narrow isthmus with broad fields sloping to the bay. There's a grocery on the right about ½ mile before the fork.

15.8 Bear left at the fork for 8.8 miles to a road on the right immediately after the Masonic Hall and Historical Society Museum on the right.

This section of the ride loops clockwise around the nothern part of the island. After a long but gradual climb, you'll enjoy a swooping downhill run to Turtle Head Cove. (Turtle Head, the extreme northern tip of the island, is private.)

24.6 Right for 2.1 miles to the first right (a sign indicates the way to the ferry).

The road hugs the water, going past well-maintained houses and fields sloping down to the bay.

26.7 Right for 1.1 miles to the ferry dock.

Final mileage: 27.8.

Bicycle Repair Services

Maine Sport, 24 Main Street, Camden (236-8797)

Oggibike, 29 Mountain Street, Camden (236-3631)

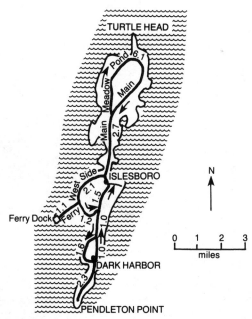

25 Bicycle Tours in Maine © 1986 Backcountry Publications

The Down East Coast

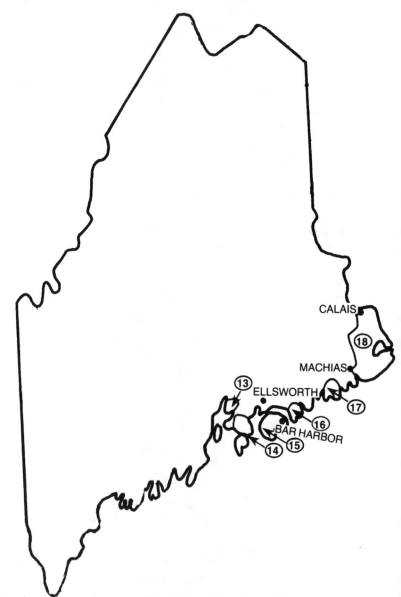

13.

Castine Ride: Orland—Castine—Penobscot

Distance: 41 miles
Terrain: Rolling, with several steep hills.
Special features: Historic sites and fine architecture in Castine, lighthouse, Maine Maritime Academy, ocean and bay views.

This is a tour of the beginning of the Down East Coast, which extends from the eastern shore of Penobscot Bay to the Canadian border. Penobscot Bay is bordered on the east by the large, triangular Blue Hill Peninsula, which extends from Bucksport and Ellsworth on the north to Stonington at the southern tip. The northwestern section of this region is a smaller peninsula with Castine at the bottom. The smaller peninsula has a different flavor than the rest of the region, seeming more mid-coastal than Down East in character. Few tourists visit Castine, so traffic on this ride is pleasantly light.

Starting from the northern tip of Penobscot Bay, the ride follows the bay shore for about 15 miles to the small head on which Castine is located. The landscape is a pleasant mix of woods and rolling farmland with views of the bay.

Castine is a quiet, gracious, unspoiled town with a tumultuous history. Founded by Plymouth Pilgrims, it changed hands between the French, British, Dutch, and American colonists before the Revolutionary War. In 1779, a fleet of nearly 40 American ships, attempting to wrest control of Castine from the British, was destroyed by them. During the mid-19th century, the town's fortune improved as shipbuilding and maritime commerce flourished. Successful sea captains and traders built elegant homes on the hillside slanting back from the bay. While bicycling through the town, you will see numerous historic markers that trace its past. You'll pass the Maine Maritime Academy, which maintains a large World War II troop ship as a training vessel.

From Castine, the route follows the Bagaduce River up the eastern side of the peninsula to the tiny village of Penobscot at the river's northern end. The route continues north, heading inland, across rolling open landscape with extensive views, and finally turns northwest back toward the start. There's a glorious downhill run approaching Route 1.

Directions for the ride

Start from the IGA supermarket on Route 1 in Bucksport. It's about a mile east of the Penobscot River bridge, and just west of Route 46.

0.0   Right (east) out of the parking lot for 0.8 mile to Route 175, which bears right.

0.8   Bear right for 8.1 miles to the point where Route 175 turns left and Route 166 goes straight.

Near the beginning of this stretch, the road drops sharply to a bridge over a stream, and then climbs steeply for 0.3 mile. Beyond, you'll follow a ridge with views of the bay in the distance, and then descend gradually to the water's edge. When you get to the intersection you can shorten the ride to 25 miles (and bypass Castine, of course), by cutting across the peninsula on Route 175.

8.9   Straight on Route 166 for 1.9 miles to the fork where Route 166 bears left and Route 166A bears right.

10.8   Bear right for 3.9 miles to the point where the main road curves right, merging onto Route 166.

Most of this section is inland from the bay, but halfway along you'll descend to the shore and climb steeply away from the water again.

14.7   Curve right on Route 166 for ½ mile to the first right, at the bottom of the hill, opposite a small cove.

15.2   Right for 1.2 miles to the end.

There's a steep 0.3-mile climb on this road. At the end, Fort George, a series of earthen embankments, is on your right. It was built by the British in 1779 and occupied until the end of the war. Opposite the intersection are the red brick buildings of the Maine Maritime Academy, with traditional collegiate architecture.

16.4   Right at the end for 1 mile to the dead end.

The road traverses a hillside sloping sharply to the bay on your left, passing handsome mansions. Just before the end, a footpath on the left leads 100 yards to a small, pine-covered point behind Dice Head Light. A wooden stairway leads down to the rocky shore. The lighthouse, built in 1829, is no longer in use.

17.4   Backtrack 0.1 mile to the first right, Perkins Street.

17.5   Right for 1 mile to a crossroads and stop sign (Pleasant Street).

The road hugs the coast, passing sea captains' homes standing guard above the waves. On your right is the brick Wilson Museum, with Indian artifacts, period furnishings, and a blacksmith shop. Beyond are two small, attractive churches, one of wood, and the other of stone.

18.5   Right for 0.1 mile to another stop sign in the center of Castine (Main Street on the left).

You'll see a concrete overlook on the right from which you can observe the *State of Maine,* the training ship of the Maine Maritime Academy. When the ship is in port it is open to the public.

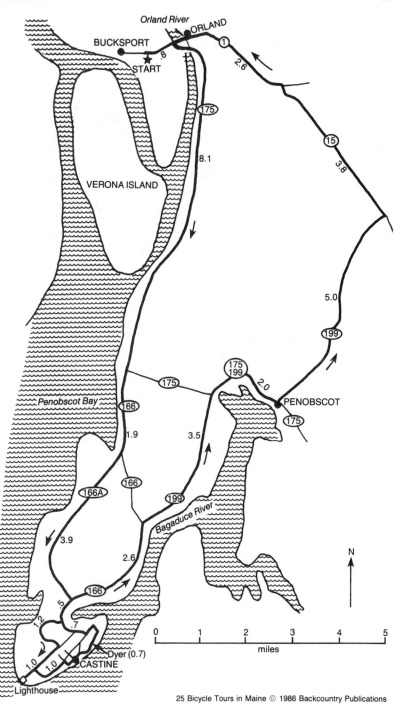

Orland River
ORLAND
BUCKSPORT
.8
START
1
2.6
175
8.1
15
3.8
VERONA ISLAND
5.0
199
175
199
175
2.0
166
Penobscot Bay PENOBSCOT
175
1.9 3.5
166
166A
199
Bagaduce River
3.9
2.6
166
N
.5
1.2 .7
Dyer (0.7)
1.0 1.0 CASTINE
Lighthouse

0   1   2   3   4   5
miles

25 Bicycle Tours in Maine © 1986 Backcountry Publications

When you get to Main Street, there's a snack bar and grocery at the intersection—the last food on the ride. Look along the street, which climbs steeply to the ornate Pentagoet Inn and a fine white church.

18.6 Straight for 0.2 mile to a fork (Dyer Street bears left uphill).

18.8 Bear right along the water. After ½ mile, the main road turns 90 degrees left at the top of the hill. Continue for 0.2 mile to the first right, State Street.
Dramatic views of the bay unfold on your left from the hilltop.

19.5 Right, up a short steep hill, for 0.2 mile to a stop sign (Route 166 North goes straight).

19.7 Continue straight on Route 166 for 3.6 miles to the fork where Route 199 bears right and Route 166 bears left.
This is an inspiring road, following a ridge high above the bay, with panoramic vistas.

23.3 Bear right on Route 199 for 5.5 miles to the point where Route 199 turns left and Route 175 goes straight, in the tiny hamlet of Penobscot.
The road is very rolling, passing through open countryside with views of the bay.

28.8 Left on Route 199 for 5 miles to the end (Route 15), at the top of the hill.
The large solitary hill to your right is Blue Hill, about 8 miles away.

33.8 Left on Route 15 for 3.8 miles to the end (Routes 1 and 3).
You'll climb steadily onto a high open ridge with views of distant hills, and then enjoy a long, fast descent to Route 1.

37.6 Left on Routes 1 and 3 for 3.4 miles to the IGA on the left.
The road is busy, but there's a wide shoulder.
Final mileage: 41.0.

Bicycle Repair Services

Gulliver's Bicycle Shop, 163 Main Street, Ellsworth (667-3223)
Bergfeld Bicycle Shop, Route 1, Searsport (548-2916)
Pat's Bike Shop, 373 Wilson Street, Brewer (989-2900)
Wilderness Sports, 33 School Street, Bangor (945-0966)

14.

The East Penobscot Tour: Blue Hill—Deer Isle—Stonington

Distance: 79 miles in 2 days (40 the first day, 39 the second). For a shorter ride which can be done as a day trip, you can take the mainland loop only (44 miles), or the Deer Isle-Stonington loop only (31 miles).

Terrain: Continuously rolling, with numerous steep hills—a challenge! The Deer Isle-Stonington loop is gently rolling with several short, steep hills.

Special features: Unspoiled small towns and fishing villages, numerous coves and inlets, reversing falls.

Accommodations: (all on Main Street, Stonington) *Captain's Quarters Inn and Motel:* 367-2420. *Boyce's Motel:* 367-2421. *Pre's Du Port Bed and Breakfast:* 367-5007.

The large, triangular peninsula between Penobscot Bay and Mount Desert Island is ideal for bicycling if you're willing to tackle a challenging landscape of continuously rolling hills. The scenery is superb: an ever-changing landscape of sheltered coves filled with lobster boats, sleepy villages, and boulder-strewn hills with dramatic views of the bay in the distance. Traffic is light as virtually all vacationers zip across the top of the peninsula on Route 1 on their way to Acadia National Park. The peninsula is divided into two distinct portions: the mainland on the north, and the island of Deer Isle, with the town of Stonington at the southern tip, on the south. The coastline of both sections is some of the most jagged in Maine, twisting around a little harbor, snaking out to a spruce-lined point and working its way back inland to the next inlet.

The ride starts from the lovely town of Blue Hill, which is on the eastern shore of the peninsula about a third of the way down. From the small town center overlooking the harbor, several roads fan outward up the neighboring hillsides, passing elegant white houses with dark shutters and fanlights above the door. Just north of the town is the round, blueberry-covered hill for which the community is named. During the summer, Blue Hill is a crafts and cultural center, with chamber music concerts at Kneisel Hall. The annual Blue Hill Fair, an authentic old-time agricultural fair, is held the last weekend of August.

From Blue Hill, the route heads west across a narrow segment of the peninsula to the Bagaduce River, a long tidal inlet. You'll cross it at Bagaduce Falls, a reversing falls popular with canoeists. The route curves south to the narrow, high-arched suspension bridge between the mainland and Deer Isle, passing through the small villages of West Brooksville and Brooksville. On Deer Isle, the ride follows an untraveled backroad along the western shore to Stonington.

Stonington, at the bottom of the island, is a classic Maine lobster port. Weathered docks on tall pilings poke into the small harbor; old warehouses and fishing shanties line the shore; and a potpourri of simple houses with peaked roofs clamber up the steep hillside behind the harbor. Plan to stay overnight here, and head up the other side of the island the next day. Once back on the mainland, the road winds through the unspoiled villages of Sargentville, Sedgwick, and Brooklin before turning north to Blue Hill. The last several miles hug the shore of Blue Hill Bay, passing Blue Hill Falls, another reversing falls.

Directions for the 79-mile ride
First Day: 40 miles
Start from Blue Hill Park, at the end of Water Street. It's south of Route 15, opposite Route 177, just past the hospital. You can leave your car at the park overnight, or at the hospital if you get permission.

0.0 Follow Water Street to Route 15, in the center of town.
The town hall, a handsome building with an arched portico, built in 1896, is on the far side of the intersection.

0.2 Bear left on Route 15 South for 0.6 mile to the crossroads at the top of the hill (Routes 172 and 175 on the left).
The hill leading out of town is a tough one. Just after you turn onto Route 15, the brick library and a white church will be on your left.

0.8 Straight for 4.2 miles to the end, where Route 15 turns left and Route 176 turns right.
The road ascends a ridge with a sweeping view.

5.0 Right for 2.4 miles to Route 175 on the left (a sign says "to Brooksville"). The landscape has a distinctive Down East flavor—a blend of scrubby woodlands and fields peppered with boulders and blueberry bushes, and not as prosperous as southern and mid-coast Maine.

7.4 Left for 1.1 miles to the end.
The road descends to the Bagaduce River, crossing it next to the reversing falls. There's a snack bar at the bridge serving delicious fried clams. At the end, Route 175 turns left and Route 176 turns right.

8.5 Turn right on Route 176. After about 10 miles, Route 176 runs head-on into Route 175, in Brooksville. Continue straight for 0.7 mile to the end.
Notice the big, weathered grange hall on your right as soon as you turn. The road weaves up and down a continuous succession of short but steep rolling hills, through farmland and blueberry fields with glimpses of the bay in the distance. After 2 miles you'll pedal into the tiny village of West Brooksville, where there's a country store and a small church standing all alone on a little rise. The road descends

delightfully into South Brooksville, another miniscule village with a cove on the right and a small store on the left, set back from the road.

Shortly before the end is Brooksville, where you can visit the Brooksville Historical Society Museum. Built in 1817, it displays farm implements, household articles, and clothing from the 18th and 19th centuries.

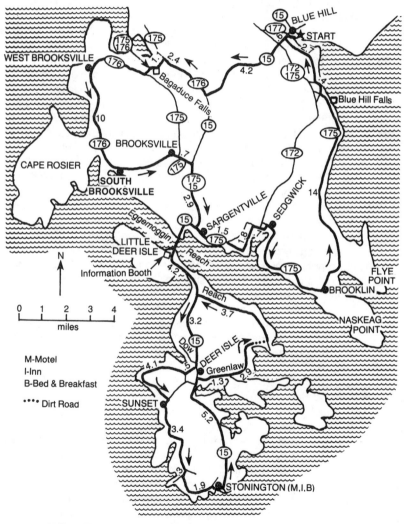

19.3 Right at the end (still Route 175) for 2.9 miles to the end.

Halfway along there's a tough climb up Caterpillar Hill, but you'll be rewarded by a dramatic view across miles of boulder-strewn blueberry moors with the bay glistening below. The rest area at the top is a great picnic spot.

When you get to the end, the long ride turns right on Route 15, and the short ride turns left on Route 175.

22.2 Right on Route 15 for 7.4 miles to an unmarked road on the right in the village of Deer Isle (a sign may point to Sunset). The road comes up just before you start to climb a hill.

The road crosses the high bridge to Deer Isle after about a mile, and goes along a causeway a mile further on.

29.6 Right for ½ mile to a fork where a smaller road bears right.

There's a grocery store on the right as soon as you turn.

30.1 Bear right for 4.1 miles to the end, in the hamlet of Sunset.

The Salome Sellers House, built around 1830, with a collection of Indian artifacts, ship models, and period furnishings, is located here.

34.2 Right for 3.4 miles to a fork where Sand Beach Road, a smaller road, bears right. It's just after Whitman Road, which also bears right.

As soon as you turn, the miniature Sunset post office is on the right. The terrain is gently rolling with some short hills. At the fork, there's a grocery on the left.

37.6 Bear right for 0.3 mile to another fork.

37.9 Bear left, uphill, for 1.9 miles to the stop sign in Stonington.

The road hugs the rocky shore, passing wharves, lobster shanties, and gaily decorated houses. The smell of fresh fish permeates the air.

39.8 Turn right immediately after the stop sign, following the harbor on your right. Go 0.2 mile to another stop sign, in the center of Stonington.

40.0 Continue straight.

Just ahead are the overnight accommodations, clustered together. The weathered, wooden commercial buildings house a fascinating variety of craft and antique shops, galleries, and old-fashioned general stores.

Second Day: 39 miles

0.0 Continue in the same direction, with the ocean on your right. Just ahead is a fork where Route 15 bears left uphill.

The street bearing right leads to the dock for the mailboat to Isle au Haut, a rockbound wooded island about 6 miles offshore, laced with hiking trails. Half the island belongs to Acadia National Park. Unless you have an off-road bicycle, the island is unsuitable for cycling— most of the road around its perimeter is loose, soft dirt.

0.0 Bear left on Route 15 for 5.2 miles to an unmarked road on the right just after a cemetery on the right. There's a gas station at the intersection.

After 0.1 mile, at the top of the hill, Route 15 curves left, but if you go straight on a smaller road for 0.6 mile you'll come to Ames Pond, a small pond smothered with pink water lilies. Further on, Route 15 bobs up and down several short, steep hills.

Blue Hill rises across an inlet of Blue Hill Bay.

5.2   Right for 1.3 miles to a fork where one road bears right and the other goes straight.

6.5   Straight (don't bear right) for 2.9 miles to the end. The last ½ mile is dirt.
           Caution: The stretch before the dirt road is bumpy—take it easy.

9.4   Left at the end for 3.7 miles to the end (Route 15).
           Caution: Sections of this road are bumpy or gravelly. This is a little-used secondary road, winding through the woods.

13.1   Right on Route 15 for 4.2 miles to the intersection where Route 15 turns left and Route 175 goes straight.
           You'll cross the bridge back to the mainland and then curse at the steep climb before the intersection.

17.3   Straight on Route 175 for 1.5 miles to a smaller road that bears right.
           You'll go through Sargentville, an attractive village with fine old houses and a white church.

18.8   Bear right for 1.8 miles to the end (Route 175 again).
           The narrow road hugs the shore of an inlet.

20.6   Right on Route 175 for 0.7 mile to the end, in Sedgwick. Route 175 turns right at the intersection.
           Notice the hilltop church 100 yards down the road on the left.

21.3   Right (still Route 175) for about 14 miles to a small crossroads shortly after the concrete arched bridge.
           After about 5 miles is Brooklin, a picturesque fishing village with a wonderful old-time general store, a three-story Oddfellows Hall, a large wooden schoolhouse, and a traditional white church built in 1853.
           Three miles past Brooklin is a small square stone enclosure, originally a cattle pound. The last few miles hug the shore of Blue Hill Bay. Next to the unique arched bridge is Blue Hill Falls, another reversing falls caused by the tide surging through the narrow inlet. This is a favorite spot for canoeists and kayakers to test their whitewater skills. The crossroads is 0.4 mile after the bridge.

35.3   Bear right for 0.4 mile to a fork.

35.7   Bear right for 2.7 miles to the end (Route 15) in Blue Hill.
           Near the end is a fine view of Blue Hill (the hill) rising across the harbor. At the end, the building with the cupola in front of you is Stevens Academy, the high school, built in 1898.

38.4   Right on Route 15 for 0.1 mile to your first right.

38.5   Bear right for 0.2 mile to the park.
           Final mileage: 38.7.

Directions for the 44-mile ride (mainland loop)

0.0   Follow the long ride through the directions for mile **19.3** of the first day. At the intersection, Route 15 turns right and Route 175 turns left.

22.2   Left on Route 175 for 1.5 miles to a smaller road that bears right.
You'll go through the attractive village of Sargentville.
23.7   Follow directions to the long ride from mile **18.8** of the second day to the
end of the tour.

Directions for the 31-mile ride (Deer Isle-Stonington loop)
Start from the information booth on Route 15 in Deer Isle, ¼ mile after the
suspension bridge, on the right.

0.0   Right (south) on Route 15 for 5.2 miles to an unmarked road on the right
in the village of Deer Isle (a sign may point to Sunset). The road comes
up just before you start to climb a hill.
5.0   Follow the long ride from mile **29.6** of the first day through the directions
for mile **9.4** of the second day, to Route 15.

Bicycle Repair Services
Gulliver's Bicycle Shop, 163 Main Street, Ellsworth (667-3223 or 1-800-400-4950)

15.
Mount Desert Island—Acadia National Park

Distance: Five suggested variations, 14 to 68 miles.
Terrain: Rolling to fairly flat.
Special features: Highest coastal mountains and headlands on the Eastern Seaboard, Somes Sound, fishing villages.

Mount Desert Island has some of the most dramatic scenery in Maine. Very simply, it's a place where the highest mountains on the Atlantic coast north of Rio de Janeiro plunge into the sea. About four million visitors come to the island each year, and most are favorably impressed unless their entire stay is fogged in.

Mount Desert Island contains nearly all (but not one hundred percent) of Acadia National Park (it's usually pronounced "dessert"; the word means "barren" in French); however, only half of the island consists of park land—the other half is privately owned.

Acadia National Park is land that is owned by the United States Government and managed by the National Park Service. The park's boundaries are highly irregular because the park land has been acquired bit by bit over a long period of time, chiefly by donation. The park contains enclaves surrounded or nearly surrounded by private land, and there are also enclaves of private land surrounded by park land. Several small pieces of the park are not on Mount Desert Island: the two largest are the tip of Schoodic Peninsula (the peninsula east of Mount Desert Island, on the far side of Frenchman Bay), and half of Isle au Haut (south of Stonington).

Bar Harbor is the largest town on Mount Desert Island. It is located on the island's northeast shore, about three miles from the National Park Visitor Center and a mile from the closest park land. Most of the island's motels, stores, restaurants, and other services are in Bar Harbor.

Much of Mount Desert's appeal stems from its small size and its lack of commercial development and exploitation. Many visitors to Acadia are surprised by how small the island is. Roughly circular in shape, it is about 13 miles wide and 16 miles long; however, it seems much larger because of its incredible wealth of scenery, and because it is nearly bisected by Somes Sound into two separate islands.

The town of Bar Harbor and the National Park Service deserve the highest commendation for limiting commercial development. Thanks to strict zoning, Bar Harbor has retained the ambiance of a pre-World War II community. There are no fast food chains here, no Holiday Inns, no condominiums, no shopping malls, no four-lane neon highways leading into town. For that, you have to go back to Ellsworth. The island's other towns are virtually unspoiled. The National Park itself has only one real commercial establishment, the tastefully designed Jordan Pond House (a restaurant).

Mount Desert Island is divided into two approximately equal-sized sections by Somes Sound, which extends from the southern coast most of the way back to the north shore. The two parts contrast dramatically in geography. The eastern half, where most of the park is located, contains most of the mountains and headlands, including the highest point, 1530-foot Cadillac Mountain. The western half is for the most part much gentler, with workaday fishing villages framed by lobster boats and docks stacked with lobster traps. Most visitors to the park do not see the western portion of the island.

Because Mount Desert is so special, it is impossible to do it justice with only one bicycle ride. At the same time, the island is so small that it is impossible to have more than two loops that do not duplicate each other to a large extent. I have therefore given directions for five rides, which do overlap in places: two on the eastern half, one on the western half, a "grand tour" covering both halves, and a carriage path ride along the dirt (but rideable) roads that are off-limits to motor vehicles.

In general, bicycling on the island is a pleasure. During the 10-week high season, from late June through Labor Day, traffic is very heavy, but the roads are wide enough to be safe, and the park is full of cyclists. An 11-mile section of the Park Loop Road is a one-way, two-lane road. To avoid traffic, simply go in the off-season. In April, May, late September, and October you'll have the island nearly to yourself, and you can enjoy its dramatic views without craning your neck around people in front of you. The Visitor Center on Route 3 is open only from May through October, but the park headquarters, on Route 233 near Eagle Lake, is open all year. The park roads are silk-smooth and well graded, with some long hills but none that are really steep, and the island's other roads are generally well maintained.

Ride A: Park Loop

Distance: 26 miles (33 with side trip up Cadillac Mountain)
Terrain: Rolling, with several long, steady hills.
Special features: Rugged coast, glacial lakes, Cadillac Mountain, museum of Stone Age antiquities, wildflower garden.
Food: None, except at Jordan Pond House, an elegant restaurant.

This ride follows Park Loop Road, which goes past the most frequently visited attractions of the park and its most rugged coastal areas. If you have time for only one ride, this is the one to do. Take as much time as you can—gaze from the overlooks, visit the museum and gardens, hike along the cliffside trails or up rugged Champlain Mountain, go down to the ocean and poke among the tidal pools to observe sea urchins and marine plants. It's not difficult to stretch the ride over most of the day—Mount Desert is too special to rush through.

Start from the Acadia National Park Visitor Center on Route 3, about 3 miles northwest of Bar Harbor.

0.0   Leave the parking lot with the Visitor Center on your right, and immediately go straight ahead on Park Loop Road. Go 3 miles to the intersection where Park Loop Road turns sharply left (a sign says "Sand Beach").

At the very beginning, there's a steep hill ½ mile long. This is the worst hill on the entire island, so don't get discouraged. From the top is a spectacular view of Frenchman Bay, dotted with islands. As you bicycle along, the barren mountains, which are immense granite rocks thinly covered with scrubby trees, loom in front of you.

The next overlook explains the cataclysmic fire of October, 1947, which destroyed most of the northeastern quarter of the island. The fire roared to the coast just south of Bar Harbor, miraculously sparing the town itself, but destroying hundreds of palatial summer estates and resort hotels that America's financial barons had built during the Gilded Age of the late 1800s. As none of them were rebuilt, the fire contributed to transforming the island from an exclusive preserve of the wealthy to a place that can be comfortably enjoyed by all. In a wonderful example of nature's regenerative powers, the burned area is now reforested, with hardwoods replacing the original pine and spruce.

3.0   Sharp left (still Park Loop Road) for 2.8 miles to a small road on the right that leads to Sieur de Monts Spring (a sign may say "Nature Center").

The spring, enclosed by a small portico, is 0.2 mile from the main road. Next to it are the Robert Abbe Museum of Stone Age Antiquities, a nature center, and the Wild Gardens of Acadia, a large collection of plants and wildflowers native to the park.

A trail climbs about 1½ miles from the spring to the top of Dorr Mountain, 1270 feet high.

6.0   From the spring, backtrack to Park Loop Road (be sure it's this road and not Route 3).

6.2   Right on Park Loop Road for 2.6 miles to a road on the left (a sign says "Schooner Head Overlook").

You'll climb along the side of Champlain Mountain, with spectacular views of the bay to your left. From the Champlain Mountain Overlook you can see Highseas, one of the few mansions to survive the 1947 fire.

From the next parking lot, the rugged Precipice Trail climbs very steeply for about ½ mile to the summit of Champlain Mountain, which towers a thousand feet above the sea. If you have time for only one hike, this is the most spectacular.

8.8   Left for 0.3 mile to the dead end, and backtrack to Park Loop Road.
At the end is a headland rising sharply from the sea. A footpath leads 0.2 mile down to the shore, where at low tide you can see a small cave hollowed into the hillside. **Caution:** The footpath ends abruptly; beyond it are wet, slippery rocks.

9.4   Left on Park Loop Road for 0.6 mile to Sand Beach on the left.
This small beach, tucked between two massive headlands, is actually composed of tiny, ground-up seashells as well as sand. The headland on the left, called Great Head, is a sheer cliff 145 feet high. Swim if you dare—the water is always freezing. An easy foot trail follows the shore for 1.8 miles from Sand Beach (from the upper parking lot, near the road) to Otter Point.

10.0 Continue for 0.7 mile to Thunder Hole, a narrow crevice in the rock with vertical walls.

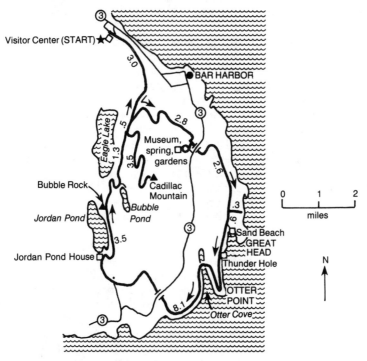

25 Bicycle Tours in Maine © 1986 Backcountry Publications

When the sea is angry, and for a brief period in the middle of the incoming tide, the waves crash into the opening, compressing the air trapped inside with a thundering boom. On calm days there is no thunder, only the soft gurgle of the sea lapping meekly against the rocks. There's a short steep hill when you leave Sand Beach.

10.7 Continue for 7.4 miles to a road on the left (a sign says "to Route 3, Blackwoods Campground, Northeast Harbor").

Here the ride goes straight, but if you're doing the Grand Tour (Ride D) turn left.

The first half of this stretch hugs the shore along dramatic Otter Cliffs, down to Otter Point, and around Otter Cove. Otter Cliffs, an unbroken wall over 100 feet high, are the highest sheer cliffs on the Eastern Seaboard. The last 2 miles of this stretch, and the remainder of the ride, head inland through woods and along glacial lakes.

18.1 At the intersection continue straight, following the sign to Jordan Pond, for 0.6 mile to the Jordan Pond House on your left.

This is an elegant restaurant, famous for tea and popovers. It replaces the original one, a farmhouse which was built in 1847 and burned in 1979. Be sure to look behind the building, where a broad lawn sweeps down to the shore of mountain-ringed Jordan Pond. Two hump-shaped hills, called the Bubbles, guard the opposite end of the pond.

18.7 Continue for 2.9 miles to a small road on the right that leads to Bubble Pond, which is just off the main road.

Bubble Pond is a smaller version of Jordan Pond, a sausage-shaped glacial lake hemmed in by granite mountains. A stream cascades from the end of the pond.

After you leave Jordan Pond House, the road climbs onto a hillside bordering the pond. Just past the pond, look to your left for Bubble Rock, a large boulder perched precariously on top of South Bubble. If you pedal furiously, you can probably get beyond it before it topples down the hill onto the road.

21.6 From Bubble Pond, continue for 1.3 miles to the road to the summit of Cadillac Mountain, on your right.

You'll ascend a hillside above Eagle Lake, the largest of the three ponds on the ride.

Side Trip: You can tackle the 3.5-mile climb to the summit of Cadillac Mountain, which at 1530 feet is the highest in the park. The road climbs steadily but not steeply to the top, gaining a thousand feet in elevation over the 3.5 miles, for an average grade of 5½ percent. (The hills at the beginning of the ride are steeper.) If you have fairly low gearing (a 32- or 34-tooth freewheel, or a 15-speed bike), and are in reasonable shape, you won't have any trouble. If you have standard 10-speed gearing (a 28-tooth freewheel) you will get to the top, but you'll push hard on the pedals, probably wanting to rest several times, and wishing you were riding in the vehicle that shares the mountain's name.

At the top, a footpath makes a short loop providing a nearly 360-degree panorama. Far below you can see Bar Harbor and the islands poised like stepping-stones across the mouth of Frenchman Bay. Just after you begin the descent, a short footpath on the right leads to Sunset Point, which provides an equally spectacular view to the west.

The descent, which is steady but not steep enough to be hairy, provides a relaxing reward for the effort of the climb. **Caution:** Take it easy on the hairpin turn halfway down.

22.9 From the bottom of the road to Cadillac Mountain, continue straight (turn right if you went to the summit) for ½ mile to a road which bears left (a sign says "to the Visitor Center").

23.4 Bear left for 3 miles to the Visitor Center.

Final mileage: 26.4.

Ride B: Jordon Pond-Seal Harbor-Northeast Harbor-Somes Sound

Distance: 23 miles.
Terrain: Rolling, with several long, steady hills.
Special features: Glacial lakes, Somes Sound, side trip to Cadillac Mountain.

This ride explores the western portion of the eastern half of Mount Desert Island, between Somes Sound and Jordan Pond. The ride starts by heading south past Eagle Lake, Bubble Pond, and Jordan Pond, which are midway between the eastern shore and Somes Sound. On the island's southern shore, the route passes through the two old-moneyed, somewhat stuffy summer colonies of Seal Harbor and Northeast Harbor. At Northeast Harbor you'll pedal north, hugging the shore of Somes Sound, with views of Saint Sauveur Mountain and Acadia Mountain rising sharply from the opposite shore. Because the ride starts by following the Park Loop Road in the opposite direction from which most visitors drive on it, traffic on this ride is much lighter than on the Park Loop ride.

Directions for the ride

Start from the Acadia National Park Headquarters on the south side of Route 233. It's 1.7 miles west of Park Loop Road, and 2.8 miles west of Route 3.

0.0 Right on Route 233, heading east, for 1.6 miles to the bridge where Route 233 passes underneath Park Loop Road.

After ½ mile, Eagle Lake will be on your right. The two hump-shaped hills at the far end of the lake are called the Bubbles.

1.7   Turn left just past the bridge, and just ahead bear left, following the sign to
          Cadillac Mountain. Go 50 yards to the end (Park Loop Road).

1.9   Turn left, heading south. After 0.4 mile Park Loop Road turns sharply left,
          but continue straight for ½ mile to the road that leads to the summit of
          Cadillac Mountain on the left.

          If you'd like to tackle the summit, it's 3.5 miles each way (see mile
          21.6 of the Park Loop ride for more detail).

2.8   Straight (left if you're coming from Cadillac Mountain) for 1.3 miles to a
          small road on the left, at the bottom of a hill, that leads to Bubble Pond
          (see mile 18.7 of the Park Loop ride for more detail).

4.1   Continue on the main road for 2.9 miles to Jordan Pond House on the
          right (see mile 18.1 of the Park Loop ride for more detail).

          Be sure to go behind the building for the view of Jordan Pond and the
          Bubbles at the far end. About a mile after leaving Bubble Pond, look
          for Bubble Rock, a large boulder perched precariously on the hillside
          on your right.

7.0   From the Jordan Pond House, continue for 0.6 mile to a traffic island
          where the road curves sharply right, at a "Yield" sign. Continue 50 yards
          to a road on the left (a sign may say "No through traffic").

7.6   Left for 0.8 mile to the end (merge right on Route 3, at a "Yield" sign), in
          Seal Harbor. A grocery and snack bar are just ahead.

8.4   Bear right on Route 3 for 3.5 miles to the end (Route 198).

          After about ½ mile you'll pass a vaulted stone Congregational church
          on the left. Beyond are some short, steep hills.

Jordan Pond and the Bubbles, Mount Desert Island.

11.9   Left at the end for 0.8 mile to a fork in the center of Northeast Harbor (Main Street bears left.)

12.7   Bear left at the fork for 0.2 mile to another fork where Kimball Road bears left and Main Street bears right.

You'll go through the center of Northeast Harbor, passing old two- and three-story wooden buildings.

12.9   Bear left on Kimball Road for 0.3 mile to the end (South Shore Road), opposite the stone church.

13.2   Turn right. After 0.4 mile the main road bears left along the water. Continue for 1.3 miles to the end (merge left at a stop sign).

South Shore Road becomes Manchester Road, passing rambling clapboard homes with wide porches standing guard above the sea.

14.9   Bear left at the end onto Sargent Drive for 3.3 miles to the end (Routes 3 and 198).

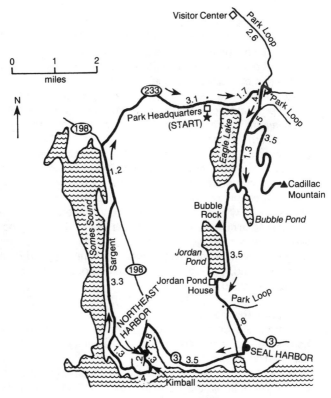

25 Bicycle Tours in Maine © 1986 Backcountry Publications

This is one of the nicest rides on Mount Desert Island, clinging to the shore of Somes Sound, with views of the rugged Saint Sauveur and Acadia Mountains, both rising to a height of 680 feet, on the far side.

18.2   Left on Routes 3 and 198 for 1.2 miles to Route 233 on the right.

Here the ride turns right, but if you're doing the Grand Tour (Ride D), go straight.

19.4   Turn right on Route 233 for 3.1 miles to the Park Headquarters on the right.

Final mileage: 22.5.

Ride C: Western Loop

Distance: 28 miles

Terrain: Gently rolling.

Special features: Echo Lake, Mount Desert Oceanarium, ocean views, fishing villages, lighthouse, side trip to Swans Island.

This ride loops around the western, and much less-visited, half of Mount Desert Island. You'll start from the attractive village of Somesville, near the northern tip of Somes Sound, and head south along Echo Lake. Like most of the other lakes on Mount Desert Island, Echo Lake is slender and hemmed in by granite mountains. Beyond is Southwest Harbor, a colorful lobster port where weathered docks with little red shacks at the end jut into the boat-filled harbor. Here you can visit the Mount Desert Oceanarium, which is a combination of an aquarium, museum, and marine learning center.

Below Southwest Harbor, the route follows the circular bulge of land that forms the southern tip of Mount Desert Island. You'll enjoy ocean views from the quiet summer community of Manset and from the natural seawall a couple of miles south. Ahead is Bass Harbor, another classic Maine lobster village that is completely uncommercial. From here you can take the 40-minute ferry ride to Swans Island. The route now skirts the largely undeveloped western shore of the island, passing through the tiny villages of Tremont and West Tremont, on lightly-traveled Route 102. Just before the end, you'll pass the northern end of Long Pond, the largest lake on the island.

Directions for the ride

Start from the Somesville Library, on the east side of Route 102, in Somesville. You can park in front of the library. Notice the lovely small dam behind it.

0.0   With your back to the library, turn left (south) on Route 102 for 5.8 miles to Clark Point Road on the left, in the center of Southwest Harbor.

Somesville is the oldest community on Mount Desert Island, dating back to 1761. Just after you start, notice the graceful white church and the fine old houses in the village.

You'll follow the shore of Echo Lake, which is two miles long, and walled in by rugged Beech Cliff towering 600 feet above the lake on the opposite shore at its southern end. Notice the isolated little cabin on the far shore about halfway along.

5.8 Left on Clark Point Road for 0.7 mile to the dead end, following the harbor on your right, and backtrack to Route 102.

Southwest Harbor is a traditional Maine fishing village. At the end of the road are a Coast Guard station and the Mount Desert Oceanarium. This is more than an aquarium; it is also a museum and learning center, with exhibits on the lobster and the lobstering industry, boatbuilding, and how fishermen and seafarers have adapted to the tides and the weather. The building was formerly an old hardware store.

7.2 Left on Route 102 for 0.7 mile to the intersection where Route 102 bears right and Route 102A (unmarked) turns left. Signs may point left to "Manset, Seawall" and "Seawall Campground."

7.9 Left for ½ mile to Alder Lane, a narrow road on the left.

8.4 Left for 1.2 miles to the end (Route 102A again).

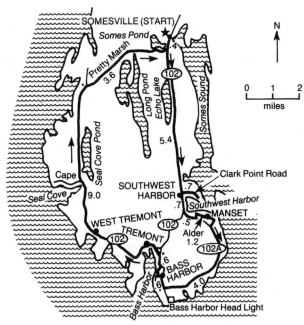

25 Bicycle Tours in Maine © 1986 Backcountry Publications

This is a lovely loop along the harbor, passing through Manset, a gracious summer community and yachting center. You'll go past the Moorings, a well-known inn and restaurant, and a good lunch spot. As you're pedaling along the water, look back over your left shoulder for a view of the harbor and the mountains rising behind it.

9.6 Left on Route 102A for 4 miles to the point where Route 102A turns 90 degrees right and a smaller road turns left.

Here the loop route turns right, but if you turn left for ½ mile you'll come to Bass Harbor Head Light, at the southernmost point of Mount Desert Island. The lighthouse, perched on top of a high craggy ledge, is a small brick tower attached to a white keeper's house. It was built in 1858. The light was automated in 1974; the keeper's house is now a private residence. Behind the lighthouse, a walkway and stairs lead down to the rocks.

13.6 Continue on Route 102A for 0.6 mile to McMullen Avenue on the left, in Bass Harbor (a sign says "to the Swans Island Ferry").

The road comes up while you're going downhill, and there's a general store on the far corner.

14.2 Left for 0.1 mile to the first right, at a stop sign.

Side Trip: Here the loop route turns right, but to go to the Swans Island ferry dock, go straight for ¼ mile. Swans Island is a pleasant spot for bicycling, with about 7 miles of paved road (there are no loops, so you have to go out and cut back on the same roads). There are three tiny settlements on the island—Atlantic, Minturn, and Swans Island. In the latter there's a museum, a marvelous general store with a snack bar, and a lighthouse at the tip of the peninsula. During the summer, several boats a day make the 40-minute crossing. The terrain on the island is hilly, but the hills are short.

14.3 Turn right (curve left if you're coming from the ferry dock) for 0.2 mile to the end (Route 102A).

14.5 Left for 0.6 mile to a road that bears left (a sign says "to Seal Cove").

15.1 Bear left for 0.3 mile to the stop sign (merge head-on into Route 102).

15.4 Straight for 8.7 miles to a fork where the main road bears right (a sign for the lefthand road says "to Pretty Marsh").

You'll go through the tiny villages of Tremont and West Tremont, which consist of a few simple houses. After 5 miles, you can bear left on Cape Road, which leads ½ mile to unspoiled Seal Cove. At the far end of the cove the road turns to dirt, so backtrack to Route 102.

24.1 Bear right at the fork for 3.6 miles to the end (Route 102).

You'll pass the northern tip of Long Pond, which is 4 miles long, and the largest lake on the island. Just before the end, Somes Pond is on the left.

27.7 Left for 0.4 mile to the library on the right.

Final mileage: 28.1

Ride D: Grand Tour

Distance: 68 miles (39 omitting the Western Loop)
Terrain: Rolling, with several long, steady hills.
Special features: Rugged coastline, Somes Sound, fishing villages, lighthouse.

Here is a tour around the entire circumference of Mount Desert Island. Starting from the Visitor Center, you'll follow Park Loop Road past the major coastal landmarks, including Thunder Hole, Sand Beach, Otter Cliffs and Otter Cove. You'll then go through Northeast Harbor and along the eastern shore of Somes Sound into Somesville. The route now follows the entire Western Loop (Ride C). To finish, you'll head north to the village of Town Hill and return to the Visitor Center along a little-used back road.

Since the route forms a figure eight, you can shorten the ride to 39 miles by omitting the Western Loop.

Because of its length, this tour is designed for the enthusiastic and experienced cyclist who would like to see most of the island's scenery on one ride, without stopping for any length of time at points of interest. The tour will be enjoyed most by cyclists who already have some familiarity with the island and its attractions.

Directions for the ride
Start from the Acadia National Park Visitor Center on Route 3, about 3 miles northwest of Bar Harbor.

0.0   Follow the Park Loop ride (Ride A) through the directions for mile **10.7**.

18.1   Turn left, following the sign for Route 3, Blackwoods Campground, Northeast Harbor. Go 50 yards, and turn left again onto an unmarked road (a sign says "No through traffic"). Go 0.8 mile to the end (merge right on Route 3 at the "Yield" sign).

18.9   Follow the Jordan Pond ride (Ride B) from mile **8.4** through the directions for mile **18.2**, to Route 233 on the right.

29.9   Continue straight on Route 198 for 1.4 miles to the end (Route 102).
There are snacks at the garage on the right. Here the Grand Tour turns left, but if you want to shorten the ride to 39 miles, turn right on Route 102 for 2.1 miles to Crooked Road on the right at the top of a hill, opposite the old wooden fire station with a bell tower (there's a country store just past the intersection).
Turn right for 4.9 miles to the end (Route 3), staying on the main road. Turn right on Route 3 for 0.4 mile to the entrance to the Visitor Center on the right.
Final mileage: 38.9.

31.3   Left on Route 102 for ½ mile to the Somesville Library on the left.
Notice the picturesque little dam behind the library.

31.8   Follow the entire Western Loop ride (Ride C).

59.9   When you arrive back at the library, continue straight on Route 102 for 2.6

miles to Crooked Road on the right at the top of a hill, opposite the old wooden fire station with a bell tower.

There's a wonderful country store just past the intersection. This is the village of Town Hill.

62.5   Right on Crooked Road for 4.9 miles to the end (Route 3).

A couple of smaller roads bear off this road, but stay on the main road. You'll pass a granite quarry shortly before the end.

A stretch of craggy coastline on Mount Desert Island.

67.4   Right on Route 3 for 0.4 mile to the entrance to the Visitor Center on the right.

Final mileage: 67.8

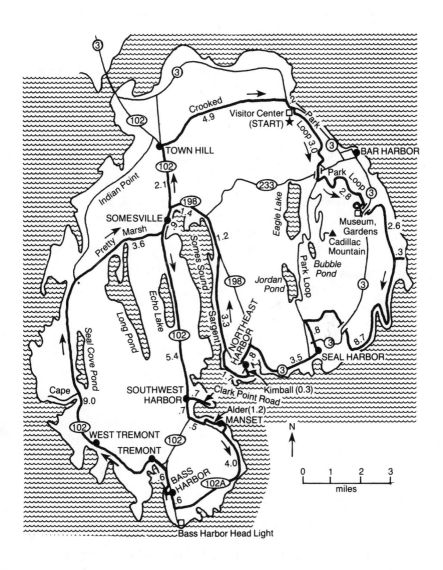

Ride E: Carriage Path Ride

Distance: 14 miles
Terrain: Gently rolling, with two long hills.
Special features: Roads off-limits to motor vehicles, Eagle Lake, Bubble Pond.
Road surface: Hard packed gravel. A mountain bike is recommended.
Caution: Although the roads are generally hard-packed, there may be loose spots. Take it easy, especially on downhill runs. Also watch for pedestrians and horses.

A unique feature of Acadia National Park is its network of dirt roads, called carriage paths, that wind through the interior forests and skirt the lakes and flanks of the mountains. The roads, on which motor vehicles are not allowed, are ideal for hiking, horseback riding, cross-country skiing, and bicycling. Construction of the 43-mile network was financed and directed by John D. Rockefeller, Jr., between 1917 and 1933. The roads are superbly engineered, with gentle grades, stone culverts, and retaining walls. The paths cross 16 graceful stone bridges, each one individually designed.

This ride follows 14 miles of carriage paths that are specially graded for bicycles. The rest of the paths, though not off-limits to cyclists, are not as hard-packed and are less safe for bicycling. The southern portion of the ride encircles Eagle Lake, the second largest lake in the park.

Directions for the ride

Start from the north end of the Visitor Center parking lot, where a dirt path heads away from the lot. There's a sign with a bicycle on it at the beginning of the path.

0.0 Follow the path away from the parking lot for ½ mile to the end.

The entire way is uphill, with some steep pitches that you'll want to walk. This is by far the worst hill on the ride, so don't get discouraged.

0.5 Left for 0.9 mile to the first left.

There's a spectacular view from the top of the hill, with Frenchman Bay in the distance.

1.4 Turn left, following the sign for Bar Harbor, Eagle Lake, and Duck Brook. Go 1 mile to the next road on the left, which crosses a bridge.

At the beginning of this section, you'll pass Witch Hole Pond on your right. When you get to the road on the left, the bridge, a stone arched span high above tumbling Duck Brook, is worth a look.

2.4 Bear slightly right for 1 mile to a fork where one road bears left and the other goes straight.

This section is mostly wooded, with a few clearings from which you can see the mountains in the distance.

3.4 Bear left, following the sign for Eagle Lake and Seal Harbor, for 1.1 miles to a road on the left immediately after you go underneath a stone bridge (Route 233). You will now loop clockwise around Eagle Lake.

4.5   Turn left, following the sign that says ''Around lake, Boat landing,'' for 2.1 miles to a fork.

As soon as you turn left, Eagle Lake is on your right. The hump-shaped mountain at the far end of the lake is Conners Nubble. Further along, the road is mostly wooded, with views of the lake between the trees. Bald hills with a thin covering of hardy green scrubs rise from the opposite shore.

6.6   Bear left at the fork, following the sign for Seal Harbor and Bubble Pond, for 0.3 mile to a paved road (Park Loop Road) that crosses the carriage path. Cross the paved road (**Caution:** limited visibility), and just ahead is a parking area with a view of Bubble Pond.

If you wish you can continue along the shore, but the road is not graded for bicycles.

6.9   From Bubble Pond, backtrack almost 0.4 mile to the fork (**Caution** again when crossing Park Loop Road).

7.3   Bear left at the fork, following the sign that says ''Around lake, Seal

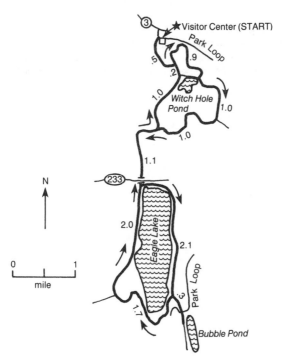

Harbor,'' for 1.7 miles to a fork where the main road curves slightly right and a smaller road bears left.

There's a long, steady climb where the road heads inland from the shore of the lake.

9.0 Continue on the main road, following the sign for Hull's Cove and Bar Harbor, for 2 miles to a stone bridge (Route 233).

There's a long, gradual descent back to the lakeshore (**Caution:** loose spots), and a lovely ride along the water. The bridge is the same one you went under earlier.

11.0 Continue underneath the bridge for 1.1 miles to the end.

12.1 Turn left, following the sign for Witch Hole and Paradise Hill, for 1 mile to the first right.

Witch Hole Pond is on the right shortly before the intersection.

13.1 Bear slightly left, following the sign for Paradise Hill and Hulls Cove, for 0.2 mile to a narrow path on the left (a sign says "to Visitor Center and Hulls Cove").

13.3 Left for ½ mile to the Visitor Center parking lot.

This is the same steep hill that you climbed at the beginning of the ride. **Caution:** The descent is steep and narrow; it's safest to walk.

Final mileage: 13.8.

Bicycle Repair Services

Bar Harbor Bicycle Shop, 141 Cottage Street, Bar Harbor (288-3886)
Acadia Bike and Canoe, 48 Cottage Street, Bar Harbor (288-5483)
Southwest Cycle, Main Street, Southwest Harbor (244-5856 or 1-800-649-5856)

16.

The Other Acadia: Schoodic Point

Distance: 29 miles
Terrain: Gently rolling, with two moderate hills.
Special features: Views of Mount Desert Island and Cadillac Mountain, Schoodic Point, fishing villages.

About 10 miles east of Mount Desert Island, on the far side of Frenchman Bay, lies an unspoiled peninsula that is ideal for a half day of bicycling. At the southern tip is Schoodic Point, a dramatic rockbound promontory that is part of Acadia National Park. There are few places in Maine off Mount Desert Island where the craggy coast is so powerfully presented. On windy days, the surf crashes onto the rocks, sending plumes of spray high into the air, in a spectacular display of nature's might. North of the point are quiet fishing villages on picturesque harbors. Another feature of the peninsula is the fine views of Cadillac Mountain across Frenchman Bay—better views than from Mount Desert Island itself.

The ride starts from West Gouldsboro, at the northwest corner of the peninsula. In the village is a Bed and Breakfast, the Sunset House (963-7156), a gracious wooden building where you might want to stay the night before the ride. Nearby are a stately white church and a handsome stone and concrete library. Halfway down the peninsula is Winter Harbor, a small fishing port at the head of an inlet filled with lobster boats. Beyond, the road clings to the coast as it works its way to Schoodic Point, and continues along the shore on the east side of the peninsula.

Halfway up the peninsula is Prospect Harbor, a classic Maine fishing village with lobster traps stacked neatly on docks with little red shacks at the far end. The last portion of the ride heads inland along the middle of the peninsula through a largely wooded area with a few small farms.

Directions for the ride
Start from the small parking area on the south side of Route 1, across from a grocery store, near West Gouldsboro. It's about 2.5 miles east of Route 183, a mile west of Route 186, and 17 miles east of Ellsworth.

0.0 Right out of the parking area, heading east, for 1.1 miles to Route 186 on the right.
1.1 Right for 3.9 miles to Fire Road 270 on the right, shortly after a church on the left. It's the second of two roads on the right about ½ mile apart.

The beginning of Route 186 follows James Cove into West Gouldsboro.

5.0 Bear right for 4.5 miles to a road on the right that goes uphill (a sign says "to Acadia National Park, Schoodic Point Section").

You'll dip down to a cove with attractive wooden houses at the water's edge, and then turn inland slightly, cutting across the top of Grindstone Neck, a wealthy summer colony. Shortly before the intersection you'll go through Winter Harbor, where there's a place to buy food and a restaurant.

9.5 Right for 4.6 miles to a fork (a sign points right to Schoodic Point).

The road hugs Frenchman Bay, with fine views of Cadillac Mountain on the opposite shore.

14.1 Bear right at the fork for 0.6 mile to the tip, where the road makes a small loop.

On a calm day, the rocks and ledges are great for picnicking, relaxing, or exploring.

14.7 Follow the main road away from the point for 5.1 miles to the end (Route 186), following the ocean on your right.

There's a grocery at the intersection. The first 3 miles cling closely to the coast.

19.8 Right on Route 186 (a fairly sharp right) for 2.1 miles to Route 195 on the left, in Prospect Harbor.

Side Trip: Here the loop route turns left, but if you go straight for 0.1 mile and turn right for 3 miles, you'll come to Corea, another unspoiled and untouristed lobster port. In the center of the village, a road on the left curls around tiny Corea Harbor. There is no place to buy food in the town.

Distinctive ledges at the tip of Schoodic Point.

21.9   Left on Route 195 (right if you visited Corea) for 5.1 miles to the end (Route 1).

      The landscape is mostly wooded, with a few small farms. This is the hilliest section of the ride, but the hills are not difficult.

27.0   Left on Route 1 for 2.3 miles to the parking area on the left, across from the grocery. This section of Route 1 has a wide shoulder.

      Final mileage: 29.3.

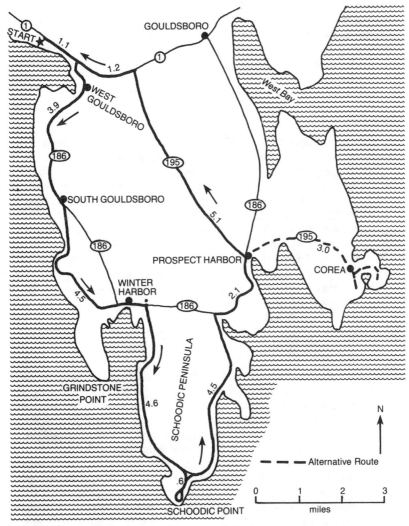

25 Bicycle Tours in Maine © 1986 Backcountry Publications

17.

Blueberries and Boats: Columbia Falls— Jonesboro—Jonesport—Addison

Distance: 43 miles
Terrain: Rolling, with a couple of tough climbs.
Special features: Ruggles House, blueberry barrens, fishing villages, bay views.
Accommodations: Since the starting point is rather isolated, you may want to stay overnight nearby before the ride. Some good spots: *Hampshire Inn,* Milbridge (546-7033). *Milbridge Inn,* Milbridge (546-7339). *Red Barn Motel,* Milbridge (546-7721).

The southwestern corner of Washington County, midway between Ellsworth and the eastern tip of Maine, is outstanding for bicycling. South of Route 1 lie unspoiled and untouristed lobster ports, and north of it is the blueberry capital of the United States, with vast blueberry fields, called barrens, stretching along broad hillsides. A pleasant feature of the area is its lack of traffic—few vacationers venture east of Ellsworth, even fewer explore the secondary roads off Route 1, while through traffic to Canada passes to the north on Route 9 and Interstate 95.

The ride starts from Columbia Falls, an attractive village of well-kept wooden houses. The Pleasant River cascades through the town and over a dam with a small hydroelectric plant next to it. A white church stands on the riverbank, and another one crowns a nearby hilltop. In the center of the village stands the Thomas Ruggles House, a superbly crafted mansion, built in 1818 for a wealthy lumber trader. The interior is splendid, with ornate woodwork and a delicate staircase which seems suspended in midair.

From Columbia Falls the ride heads northeast on a country road that quickly leads into blueberry country, ascending onto a ridge with spectacular views. You'll run parallel to Route 1 on another back road into Jonesboro, a quiet village about nine miles east of Columbia Falls. The remainder of the ride follows the perimeter of the two-pronged peninsula, with Jonesport at the bottom of the eastern part and South Addison at the tip of the western one. The ride along the eastern shore to Jonesport is a delight, with numerous views of the bay across rolling fields of blueberries.

Jonesport is a rarely visited lobster port complete with a boat-filled harbor, wharves supported by tall pilings, and weathered lobstermen's sheds and fish processing plants. The shrill cry of seagulls pierces the air while you're pedaling through the town. For a side trip, you can cross the bridge to Beals Island, where the smaller village of Beals is another classic Maine fishing community.

From Jonesport you'll follow the western half of the peninsula to Addison, a sleepy, somewhat dilapidated village which is not as prosperous as Jonesport. From Addison it's a short hop back to Columbia Falls.

Directions for the ride

Start from the post office in the center of Columbia Falls, parking at the far end of the lot, near the river. Columbia Falls is about 40 miles east of Ellsworth and just south of Route 1. From either the west or the east, a road bears off Route 1 for about ½ mile into the village.

0.0 Right out of the lot, crossing the bridge over the Pleasant River.

If you'd like to visit the Ruggles House first, turn left out of the lot for 0.1 mile; it will be on your right.

0.0 Immediately after the bridge, turn left for 0.2 mile to Route 1, at the stop sign.

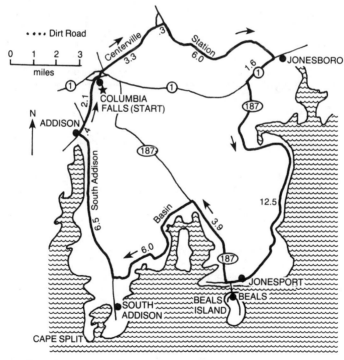

25 Bicycle Tours in Maine © 1986 Backcountry Publications

0.2   Straight for 3.3 miles to a fork where one road bears left and the other goes straight.

      You'll climb steadily through extensive blueberry barrens, followed by a sharp downhill with a great view.

3.5   Straight (don't bear left) for 0.3 mile to the end.

3.8   Right for 6 miles to the end (Route 1), in Jonesboro.

      You'll traverse open blueberry fields with sweeping views. In the spring, some of the fields are burned to fertilize the soil and keep the bushes low.

9.8   Right on Route 1 for 1.6 miles to Route 187 on the left.

      On the right, you'll pass a grocery store with a lunch counter.

11.4   Left for about 12.5 miles to the bridge to Beals Island (Bridge Street) on the left, in Jonesport.

      There's a snack bar and grocery store in town. Fine views of the bay abound on this stretch. It's worth crossing the bridge to Beals Island. At the far end of the bridge, turn either right or left. If you follow (or chase, as the local people say) the road on the left for a mile, you'll come to a short causeway to Great Wass Island, which sports a network of hiking trails. If you're lucky, you may spot an osprey or even an eagle, which occasionally are seen in the vicinity.

24.0   Continue on Route 187. After ¼ mile, it turns 90 degrees right. Continue on Route 187 for 3.9 miles to an unmarked road on the left. (As soon as you turn onto this road, a sign says "to South Addison").

      Shortly before the intersection there's a grocery on the right.

28.2   Left for 6 miles to the end, at a "Yield" sign (merge right).

      This section is not as prosperous as most of the Maine coast. At the end the ride bears right, but if you turn left for 1.5 miles you'll come to South Addison, a tiny settlement of weathered houses, a little church, and lobster traps everywhere.

34.2   Bear right for 6.5 miles to the end, in Addison.

      This is a lovely narrow road, hugging the bay as it approaches the village. Just before the end, notice the old Masonic temple on the left.

40.7   Right for 0.4 mile to a fork where one road bears left and the other goes straight.

41.1   Straight for 2.1 miles to the end, in Columbia Falls (merge right at "Yield" sign).

      There's a country store at the intersection. The Ruggles House is on the left on the far side of the intersection.

43.2   Bear right for 0.1 mile to the post office on the right.

      Final mileage: 43.3.

Bicycle Repair Services

Western Auto, Jonesport (497-5544)

18.

Washington County Tour

Distance: 147 miles in three days: 48 miles the first day, 51 the second, and 48 the third.

Terrain: Gently rolling, with occasional hills. This is the easiest of the overnight tours.

Special features: Roosevelt summer home, lighthouse, highest tides in the United States, easternmost point in the United States, fishing villages.

Accommodations: Night before the tour, in Machias: *Sea Gull Motel* 255-3033). *Bluebird Motel* (255-3332). *Mainland Motel* (255-3334). *Margaretta Motel* (255-6500).

First Night, in Lubec: *Home Port Inn* (Bed and Breakfast, 733-2077), *Eastland Motel* (&33-5501). *Bayviews Bed and Breakfast* (733-2181). *Peacock House Bed and Breakfast* (733-2403).

Second Night, in Calais: *International Motel* (454-7515). *Calais Motor Inn* (the fanciest, 454-7111).

ʼ

Washington County, at Maine's eastern tip, captures the spirit of the phrase "Down East." It is a remote and unspoiled land of great natural beauty. Along its coast, which is washed by the highest tides in the country, lie quiet fishing ports that rarely see visitors. Along the harbors are lobstermen's shanties and fish-processing plants, not boutiques and craft shops. Lobster boats and skiffs crowd the bays and inlets, not sailboats and yachts. Inland lies a nearly unpopulated wilderness of pristine lakes, endless forests, and blueberry fields.

Bicycling in Washington County is a pleasure. The traffic, even on Route 1, is never heavy because very few visitors to Maine come east of Ellsworth, and there are no cities or even big towns in the county. Calais, the largest town, has a population of only about 4,000. Travelers on the way to New Brunswick generally take Route 95 to Houlton or Route 9, which is not on the tour, east out of Bangor. The region's most visited attraction, Roosevelt Campobello International Park, is rarely crowded. Cyclists will also appreciate the fact that the land near the coast is not very hilly. People in the towns are friendly and may well start a conversation with you; this happened to me several times while I was exploring the area.

The tour starts from Machias (rhymes with "the bias"), an attractive town dominated by the graceful spire of the Congregational Church. The

Machias River flows through the town, crashing over a waterfall just below Route 1. The Burnham Tavern, a handsome yellow building with a gambrel roof that was built in 1770, is the oldest building in Maine east of the Penobscot River. A branch of the University of Maine is also located in town.

From Machias you'll follow the coast to Quoddy Head State Park, which contains the most easterly point of land in the United States. The park commands a pine-rimmed headland with footpaths winding along the jagged, rocky shoreline. Adjoining the park is the candy-cane-striped West Quoddy Head Light, which was built in 1808.

From the park it's about seven miles to Roosevelt Campobello International Park, which is located on Campobello Island in New Brunswick. The Island is linked to Lubec, Maine, by a bridge. In the park is Franklin Delano Roosevelt's summer "cottage," a graceful maroon mansion overlooking Cobscook Bay. The park, which is meticulously landscaped and shaded by stately groves of trees, exudes an aura of contentment and tranquillity.

From Campobello Island, the route crosses the bridge back to Maine and follows the state's easternmost coastline north to Calais (rhymes with Dallas), skirting Cobscook Bay and then the wide tidal estuary of the Saint Croix River, which separates Maine and New Brunswick. Calais is a busy little town with some fine old houses on Route 1 overlooking the river and a traditional Victorian business block of three-story brick buildings. The last segment of the tour goes from Calais southwest back to Machias, passing through a primarily wooded landscape punctuated with undeveloped lakes and occasional blueberry fields.

Directions for the ride

First day: Machias to Lubec (48 miles)

Start from the junction of Routes 1 and 92 in Machias, just west of the center of town. You'll probably stay at a motel the night before the tour. When you make your reservation, explain that you'll be taking a bicycle trip and that you'd like to leave your car there for a few days. The Sea Gull Motel is closest to the start of the ride, just east of town, on Route 1, and is reasonably priced. The Bluebird Motel is a mile west of town on Route 1. The Maineland Motel, Margaretta Motel, and Riverview House are a mile east of town, all on Route 1.

If you wish, you can leave your car at the Sheriff's office on Court Street (Route 1A), ¼ mile off Route 1, and on the right as you're heading up the hill. The officer on duty will tell you where to put the car.

A good spot to eat before and after the tour is Helen's Restaurant, which has been a Down East landmark for half a century. The original restaurant is in the center of town; a newer addition with longer hours is ½ mile east on Route 1, on the river.

0.0   Head east on Route 92 for 3.1 miles to the first left (a fairly sharp left).

West Quoddy Head Light, Lubec—easternmost point of the United States mainland.

Route 92 follows the south bank of the Machias River, south of Route 1. As you start down this road, you'll see a small electric substation on the left. Immediately after it there's a good view of the falls.

Side Trip: When you get to the road on the left the tour turns here, but if you continue straight for a mile you'll come to Machiasport, a village of well-kept houses that overlook the mouth of the river. The Gates House, a Federal-style house built in 1807, is open to the public. A mile beyond Machiasport is Fort O'Brien, on the shore of Machias Bay, where the first naval encounter of the American Revolution took place, in 1775. Only the earthworks remain.

3.1 Sharp left for 1 mile to the end (merge right at a "Yield" sign).

4.1 Bear right for ½ mile to the end (merge right on Route 1).
The road hugs the East Machias River.

4.6 Bear right on Route 1 for 0.7 mile to the first right (a sign says "to the Naval Communications Unit, Cutler").

5.3 Turn right. Just ahead, on the far side of the bridge, the main road curves right. Continue for less than 0.2 mile to the end (Route 191).

5.6 Right for about 24 miles to a road on the right near the top of a steep hill.
There's a tiny country store with a gasoline pump at the intersection. Route 191 is a nearly deserted road that is ideal for bicycling. After a few miles you'll hug the shore of Holmes Bay. The opposite shore is dominated by the forest of 26 radio towers belonging to the Naval Communications Unit, which is one of the most powerful radio stations in the world.

After about 12 miles you'll come to the lovely fishing village of Cutler, with its small harbor filled with lobster boats and lined with wharves propped up on tall pilings. Here, and on the rest of the tour as you work your way along the coast, these tall wharves are a standard feature of the landscape. Because the tides are so high, averaging over 15 feet, the docks have to be high enough so that the boats won't become grounded at low tide. There's a grocery in Cutler. Beyond the village, the road heads inland through an uninhabited landscape of scrubby evergreens and broad blueberry fields.

When you come to the road on the right, the ride turns here. This road contains a 3-mile section of dirt. If you want to avoid the dirt section (adding 4 miles to the ride, and covering ground over which you'll have to backtrack later), continue straight for 2.8 miles to the end (Route 189); turn right for 4.2 miles to a road on the right with a grocery on the far corner (a sign will say "to Quoddy Head State Park"); turn right for 2.7 miles to a fork; and bear left for 2 miles to the State Park and West Quoddy Head Light.

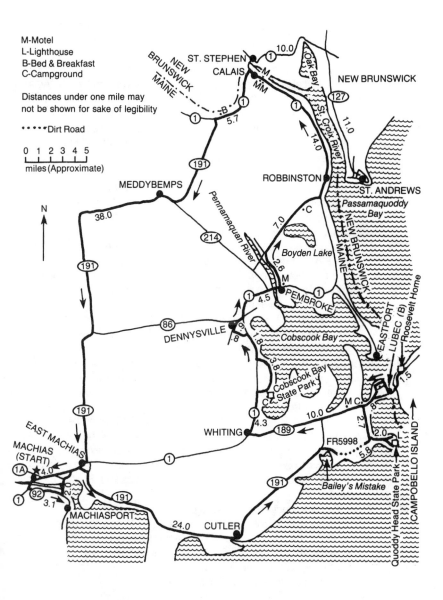

M-Motel
L-Lighthouse
B-Bed & Breakfast
C-Campground

Distances under one mile may
not be shown for sake of legibility

• • • • • Dirt Road

0 1 2 3 4 5
miles (Approximate)

N

29.6   Turn right. After 1.4 miles the road turns to dirt, a stretch that lasts for 3 miles.

Caution: Watch for rough, loose spots, especially going up or down hills. When the road becomes paved again, continue 1.4 miles to the end (merge left at a "Yield" sign). At the beginning of this road, you'll go along a small bay called Bailey's Mistake.

This colorful name commemorates a navigational error. According to legend, in 1830 a sea captain named Bailey was fogged in while sailing his schooner from eastern Maine to Boston. He attempted to land at Lubec but entered Bailey's Mistake instead and ran aground. Rather than face an embarrassing arrival in Boston, the crew settled along the shore, building houses from the ship's cargo of lumber.

35.4   Sharp right, following the water on your left, for 2 miles to a dirt fork.

To the left is West Quoddy Head Light, with its distinctive red and white candy stripes. To the right is Quoddy Head State Park, a superb picnic spot. Campobello Island lies across the channel.

37.4   From the park and lighthouse, follow the main road for 4.7 miles to the end (Route 189), just outside of Lubec.

The tour now heads to the Roosevelt home, which is 3 miles away, and open until 5 p.m. Eastern time (6 p.m. in Canada). If you don't have time to visit it now, go tomorrow.

42.1   Right on Route 189 for 0.8 mile to a fork (Route 189 bears right).

Just after you turn, a museum of the sardine industry, which was most active early in the century, is on the right.

42.9   Bear right at the fork for 0.4 mile to the bridge to Campobello Island.

On the far side of the bridge, you will go through Canadian customs. Continue for 1.5 miles to the Roosevelt Campobello International Park on the left.

Roosevelt spent summers here from 1883, when he was a year old, to 1921, when he was stricken with polio. Behind the mansion a lawn slopes down to the bay, where there's a small dock. Next to the Roosevelt home is the Hubbard Cottage, a graceful mansion with a broad porch, built in 1891 for Gorham Hubbard, a Boston insurance broker.

45.3   From the park, backtrack to the bridge.

After ½ mile, a road on the right leads 0.3 mile to Friar's Head, a dramatic headland with a tall, detached pinnacle of rock at its outer end. Go through United States customs on the far side of the bridge.

47.3   Turn right immediately after the customs office, following the water on the right, for 0.8 mile to the end (Route 189).

Caution: Watch for bumpy spots. The road loops counterclockwise around the small peninsula on which Lubec is located. At the beginning, you'll go through the center of town, which has a derelict, windswept look, and pass the Peacock Canning Company, one of the two sardine canneries in Lubec. At the turn of the century there were 20 canneries in operation. Just ahead you'll pass some abandoned fish-processing plants and Booth Fisheries, which is still alive and well. Bayviews Bed and Breakfast is at the end.

When you get to the end, the route turns right, but if you turn left for a couple of blocks there are two more Bed and Breakfasts, the Home Port Inn and the Hügel Haus. The Eastland Motel is 2.3 miles to the right, on Route 189. Ray's Seaview Restaurant, about a mile to the right on Route 189, is a good place to eat.

Final mileage (to Route 189): 48.1.

Second day: Lubec to Calais (51 miles)

0.0   From Lubec, head west on Route 189 for about 11 miles to the end (Route 1), in Whiting.

From the Eastland Motel, it's about 8.5 miles to Route 1.

11.0   Right for 4.3 miles to an unmarked road on the right (a sign says "to Cobscook Bay State Park").

As soon as you turn onto Route 1, there's a grocery on the right.

15.3   Right for 3.8 miles to the end (Route 1 again).

After ½ mile you'll pass the entrance to Cobscook Bay State Park, a lovely wooded area with trails along the bay. Cobscook Bay boasts the highest tides in the country, averaging 24 feet. It's fascinating to stand by the water's edge and visibly watch the tide come in, like a bathtub filling up. Further along the road there's a marine research station, part of Suffolk University, not open to the public.

19.1   Right on Route 1 for 1.8 miles to an unmarked road on the left (a sign says "to Dennysville").

20.9   Left for 0.8 mile to the end, immediately after the bridge.

21.7   Right for 0.9 mile to Route 1.

You'll go through Dennysville, a village with elegant houses on the hillside on the left, and the Dennys River flowing along the road on the right. You'll pass a country store and a war memorial statue, and when you come to Route 1 there's a snack bar on the right. Just before Route 1 on the left is the Lincoln House, a square yellow mansion that was built in 1787 and is now an inn.

22.6   Left on Route 1 for 5.6 miles to the second crossroads, which comes up while you're going downhill. It's 1 mile after Route 214.

28.2   Left for 2.6 miles to the first right, which crosses a bridge.

Just before the intersection there's a small dam on the right.

30.8   Bear right across the bridge for 7 miles to the end (Route 1).

After going along Boyden Lake, you'll tackle a couple of short, steep hills and then a long, steady climb onto a ridge. At the top is a great view, with Passamaquoddy Bay far below. You'll enjoy a swooping descent from the ridge. Just before Route 1 there's a grocery on the left.

37.8   Left on Route 1 for about 13.5 miles to the cluster of motels as you come
into Calais.

This is a beautiful stretch hugging the Saint Croix River. After 2 miles
you'll go through Robbinston, a lovely town with some ornate
Victorian houses and two fine churches.

About 3 miles beyond Robbinston you'll see a sign for the Saint
Croix Island International Historic Site, an overlook on the riverbank.
(To get there, turn right on the side road and immediately right down
the steep driveway to the river.) The island, named because it is in the
shape of a cross, was the site of one of the first attempts to set up a
colony in the New World. In 1604 the French sent 120 colonists to the
island, but during the severe winter, 35 died, and the survivors
resettled in Nova Scotia the following spring. As you come into
Calais, gracious old houses stand above the riverbank on Route 1.

Final mileage: 51.3.

Third day: Calais to Machias (48 miles)

0.0   From the motel, continue on Route 1 for 0.6 mile to the traffic light in the
center of Calais (Route 1 turns left here).

You'll go past a park with an old wooden bandstand on the left. Just
before the light, the attractive beige brick library, built in 1892, is on
your right overlooking the river.

0.6   Left at the traffic light (still Route 1) for 5.7 miles to Route 191 on the left (a
sign says "to Machias").

The road skirts the Moosehorn National Wildlife Refuge, a 22,000-
acre preserve of bogs, marshes, and forest.

6.3   Left on Route 191 for about 38 miles to Route 1, in East Machias.

After about 8 miles you'll pass through the tiny village of Meddybemps, which contains only a few houses and a country store. As you
come into the village, Meddybemps Lake is on the right, about 100
yards off the road. Beyond Meddybemps the land is mostly wooded,
with occasional blueberry fields. It also gets hillier.

About 8 miles after Meddybemps there's a long climb onto a
ridge with a view of Lake Cathance in the distance. The road
descends to the lake and follows it, but the view of the water is
blocked by the trees. Beyond the lake the terrain is moderately hilly,
and mostly wooded.

44.3   Right on Route 1 for 4 miles into Machias.

Final mileage: 48.3.

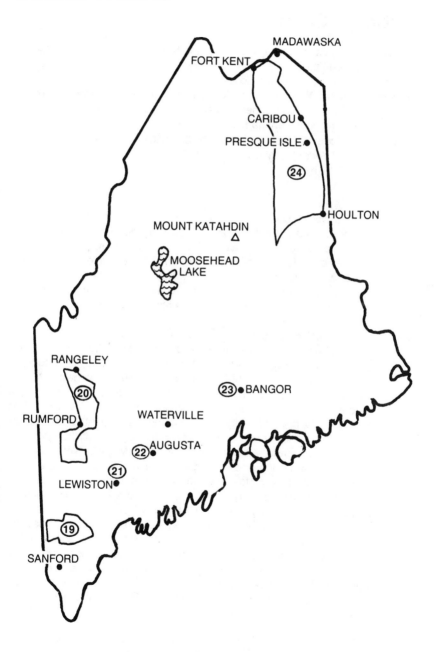

Inland Maine

19.

Sebago Century

Distance: 99 miles in two days: 59 miles the first day, 40 the second. You can also complete this ride in one day.

Terrain: Rolling, with several difficult hills.

Special features: Willowbrook at Newfield (living history museum), covered bridges, Hiram Falls, Jones Gallery of Glass and Ceramics, Douglas Mountain Preserve, Sebago Lake.

Accommodations: *Cornish Inn,* Cornish (625-8501). *Mid-Way Motel,* Cornish (625-8835). *York County Campground,* Cornish (625-8808).

When bicycling became popular in 1880, a ride of a hundred miles, quickly dubbed a Century, became a challenge. Nearly every bicycle club in the country incorporates a Century into its ride schedule, and as a rule, the ride is done in one day. However, it's a lot more enjoyable in two, especially if there are places along the way that are worth visiting. If you really want to tackle this ride in one day, you can do it if you get into shape first, but you won't have time to see the attractions along the way.

The countryside between the western suburbs of Portland and the New Hampshire border is ideal for bicycling, with prosperous rolling farmland, unspoiled small towns, and quiet lakes. Dramatic mountain views unfold near the New Hampshire border. At the region's northern edge is the broad sweep of Sebago Lake, the second largest in Maine. The area contains a surprising number of places to see, including a restored 19th-century village, an outstanding museum of antique glass and ceramics, covered bridges, and a hilltop preserve with a spectacular view. With no cities or even large towns in the region, traffic is light, even on numbered roads. Although this portion of Maine is very rural, an extensive network of paved secondary roads, as fine as anywhere in the state, allows the bicyclist to come into intimate contact with the landscape.

The ride starts from Gorham, a small rural town 10 miles west of Portland. As soon as you head west you will see prosperous farming country with big white farmhouses and rustic old barns. After passing through the attractive little towns of Bar Mills, Hollis Center, and Limerick, you'll arrive at Willowbrook at Newfield, a living history museum of a rural community during the late 1800s. Among its numerous restored buildings, staffed by guides in period costume and working at traditional crafts, are several houses with authentic furnishings, a machine shop, a cider mill, and a bicycle shop.

Beyond Willowbrook, the route turns north, paralleling the New Hampshire border about three miles away. This is the hilliest section of the tour, but you'll be rewarded by hillside views and exhilarating downhill runs. After crossing the old covered bridge into Porter, you'll follow the Ossipee River to the fine old town of Cornish, where you can spend the night at either a charming country inn, a standard motel, or a campground.

Just three miles from Cornish is Hiram Falls, a dramatic dam-plus-falls on the Saco River with a 75-foot drop. Above the falls stands a hydro-electric plant. The Saco, a favorite of canoeists, is southern Maine's major river, slicing from New Hampshire's White Mountains to the ocean at Biddeford and Saco. About 10 miles further on is the Jones Gallery of Glass and Ceramics, a superb collection of antique glassware and china from all over the world and from all periods of history. An unusual feature of the gallery is a separate exhibit of items with imperfections or of limited artistic merit. Adding to the museum's charm is its location on a lonely mountain road. A footpath leads from the Jones Gallery to the top of Douglas Mountain, from which a magnificent view sweeps from Sebago Lake to the White Mountains.

A fast descent brings you to Sebago Lake, which is about seven miles across and 10 miles long. Only 25 miles northwest of Portland, it is a favorite spot for vacationers, with hundreds of cabins nestled in the woods along its shore. The lake is also the source of Portland's water supply, which has prevented the onslaught of development. The route runs parallel to the lake for several miles along its southwest shore. From Sebago Lake it's about 11 miles back to Gorham. Once again you'll roll through wide expanses of farmland and cross another covered bridge.

Directions for the ride
First day: 59 miles

Start from the Park and Ride lot on Route 25 in Gorham. It's 0.8 mile east of the center of town, and 1.5 miles west of Route 237.

From the Maine Turnpike, take Exit 8 and follow the signs to Route 25 and Westbrook. Park at the back of the lot, on the dirt. The lot is behind the police station; you should tell the police that you'll be leaving your car overnight.

0.0   Right out of the parking lot, heading west, on Route 25 for 0.8 mile to Route 114, at the traffic light in the center of Gorham.

Just before the light is a restaurant where you can have breakfast.

0.8   Straight for 0.4 mile to Flaggy Meadow Road, which bears left.

1.2   Bear left for 0.6 mile to a crossroads (Cressy Road), at the blinking light.

1.8   Straight for 1.7 miles to Waterman Road, which bears left.

It's immediately after Webster Road on the right, just before the top of the hill. The road ascends onto a low ridge with a good view and passes through a mixture of woods and farmland.

3.5   Bear left for 1.2 miles to a fork where one road bears left and the other
           (Carl Road) goes straight.
4.7   Straight on Carl Road for 0.7 mile to the end.
5.4   Left for 0.8 mile to the end (Route 22).
6.2   Left for 0.2 mile to the first right (Rankin Road).
6.4   Right for 1.9 miles to the end (Route 112), passing through farmland.
8.3   Left for 0.4 mile to the traffic light (Route 4A), in Bar Mills.
           There's a grocery on the corner.
8.7   Right on Route 4A for 0.4 mile to a fork where the main road bears left
           across the bridge over the Saco River.
9.1   Bear left for 2.2 miles to a crossroads (Route 117).
           Notice the old factory on the right while crossing the bridge.
11.3   Turn right. Just ahead you'll cross Route 35. Continue on Route 117 for
           2.6 miles to a crossroads (Pleasant Hill Road on the left).
14.0   Left on Pleasant Hill Road for 1.3 miles to the end (Killock Hill Road).
15.3   Right for less than 0.2 mile to Whitehouse Road on the left.
15.5   Left for 1 mile to the end.
           You'll have a tough hill ¼ mile long, followed by a well-earned
           descent.
16.5   Left for 3.9 miles to a crossroads (Route 5) and stop sign.
20.4   Right for 8.5 miles to Route 11 on the left, at a blinking light, as you come
           into Limerick.
           There's a grocery and snack bar as soon as you turn, and another
           grocery after 3 miles. At the beginning of this stretch you'll follow the
           shore of Little Ossipee Pond. Just past the second grocery store,
           notice the fine stucco church on the left. Just before Limerick, there's
           another attractive church at the top of the hill.
              When you get to Route 11 the ride turns left, but just ahead is the
           center of Limerick and a food store. At the intersection, notice the
           Federal-style house and the Gothic-style church.
28.9   Left on Route 11 for 0.4 mile to the point where Route 11 curves left and a
           smaller road (Old Newfield Road) goes straight.
29.3   Straight on the smaller road for 1.2 miles to a fork.
30.5   Bear left for 2.9 miles to the end (Route 11), in Newfield.
           Several roads bear off the main road on both the right and the left, but
           stay on the main road at each intersection. Shortly before the end is
           Willowbrook at Newfield. The main building, the William Durgin
           Homestead, built in 1813, is on the left.
33.4   Right on Route 11 for 3.1 miles to the intersection where Route 11 turns
           left and Route 110 goes straight.
36.5   Straight for 0.9 mile to the crossroads where Route 110 turns left.
           There's a country store on the corner.
37.4   Right at the crossroads for 5.3 miles to a fork where the main road curves
           sharply left and a smaller road bears right.
           There's a church at the intersection. This stretch is very hilly but beau-

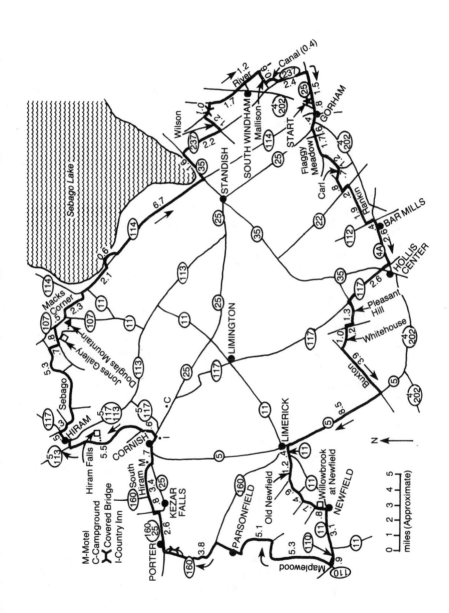

tiful, with fields crisscrossed by stone walls, old barns and rambling farmhouses, and views of wooded hills across the pastures. You'll pass through the tiny community of Maplewood, with a little post office and weathered grange hall.

42.7 Continue on the main road for 5.1 miles to the end (Route 160).

The hilly but inspiring landscape continues through the township of Parsonfield. After 3 miles, you'll see a stately white church on the left. There's a difficult climb after the church, but you will be rewarded by a sweeping view and a wild descent to Route 160.

47.8 Turn left on Route 160. After 1.2 miles, the main road curves 90 degrees right. Continue for 2.6 miles to the end (Route 25), in Porter.

Just after the 90-degree turn, the graceful white buildings of the Parsonfield Seminary will be on your right. Shortly before the end, you'll cross the Ossipee River. To your right is the Porter Bridge, a covered bridge built in 1876. If you wish, you can bear right just before the river and cross the covered bridge instead of the new one.

51.6 Right on Route 25 for 2.6 miles to the crossroads, where Route 160 turns left and Route 25 turns right, in Kezar Falls.

There's a country store on your left as soon as you turn. The road hugs the Ossipee River on the right. At the end the loop tour turns left, but if you turn right you'll cross the river into the center of Kezar Falls, an attractive small town. As you cross the river there's a dam on the right and an old mill on the left. Just past the bridge is a store and a snack bar.

54.2 Turn left on Route 160 and just ahead turn right, staying on Route 160. Go 0.8 mile to the point where Route 160 turns left and another road goes straight.

55.1 Straight for 3.4 miles to the end (merge left on Route 25).

The Mid-Way Motel is on the left just before the end.

58.5 Bear left on Route 25 for 0.7 mile to Bridge Street, which bears left opposite the Cornish Inn.

Notice the handsome brick library on the left on the far side of the intersection and the distinctive white church on the right just beyond the Inn. If you'd like to camp, continue on Route 25 for about 2 miles to the York County Campground on the left.

Final mileage to the Inn: 59.2.

Second day: 40 miles

0.0 Bear left on Bridge Street opposite the Inn, passing the library on your right, for 0.6 mile to a fork.

0.6 Bear slightly right for 5.5 miles to a crossroads and stop sign (Routes 5 and 113), in Hiram.

After 3.2 miles, look for a dirt path on the right with some granite blocks where it joins the road, just as you start to go uphill. The path

A dam on the Ossipee River, Kezar Falls.

leads about 200 yards to Hiram Falls, also called Great Falls. At times the dam prevents the water from flowing over the falls.

6.1 Turn right, cross the bridge, and bear left on Route 117 North for ½ mile to a crossroads.

There's a country store here.

6.7 Right at the crossroads for 0.3 mile to a fork. Ignore a very small road that bears right shortly before the fork.

7.0 Bear slightly right for 5.3 miles to the third paved right, Orchard Road, almost at the top of a hill.

12.3 Right for 0.7 mile to the end.

This road climbs steadily through orchards. As you're climbing, look back for a great view.

13.0 Left for 100 yards to Douglas Mountain Road, which bears right.

13.1 Bear right for 0.1 mile to the Jones Gallery of Glass and Ceramics on the right.

If it's a clear day be sure to walk the ½ mile to the top of Douglas Mountain, from which there's an inspiring view of Sebago Lake and the White Mountains. From the Gallery, continue up the road for ¼ mile to a small dirt parking lot on the left. (It's easier to walk than to bicycle up the steep grade.) Turn left onto a footpath for ¼ mile to the top. At the top there's a stone observation tower and a monument inscribed "Non sibi sed omnibus"—Latin for "Not for one but for all."

13.2 From the Gallery, backtrack 0.1 mile to the main road.

13.3 Sharp right for 0.8 mile to the end, at the bottom of the hill (merge right on Route 107).

Caution: This is a steep downgrade that ends suddenly while you're still going downhill.

14.1 Bear right on Route 107 for ½ mile to a fork where Route 107 bears right.

14.6 Bear left for 2.3 miles to the end (Route 114).

You'll enjoy a gentle descent.

16.9 Right for 2.1 miles to Wards Cove Road, a smaller road that bears left along the shore of Sebago Lake.

Notice the fieldstone library on the right shortly after you turn.

19.0 Bear left on Wards Cove Road for 0.6 mile to the end (Route 114 again).

This is a delightful ride along the lake, passing rustic cottages.

19.6 Left on Route 114 for 6.7 miles to a crossroads (Route 35) and blinking light.

A grocery store and a pizza shop are at the corner.

26.3 Left on Route 35 for 1.6 miles to Route 237 on the right.

The road follows the lakeshore through pine groves.

27.9 Right on Route 237 for 2.2 miles to a crossroads (Wilson Road) at the top of a short hill.

30.1 Left for 1.2 miles to the end.

Notice the old grange hall on the right as soon as you turn. The road rolls past large farms.

31.3 Right for 1 mile to the end (Hurricane Road).

You'll cross the covered bridge, called Babb's Bridge, that spans the Presumpscot River. It is a replica of the original one, which was built in 1864 and burned in 1973.

32.3 Right for 1.7 miles to a crossroads (Routes 202 and 4), at the blinking light.

34.0 Straight (**Caution** here) for 1.2 miles to the second right (Mallison Street), at the bottom of the hill.

This is a pleasant ride through broad sweeps of farmland.

35.2 Right for 0.6 mile to Canal Street on the left, immediately after the bridge.

You'll pass the Maine Correctional Center. At the bridge, notice the dam and the old brick mill on the left.

35.8 Left for 0.4 mile to the end (merge left on Route 237).

There's a nasty little hill on this road, the last hill of the tour.

36.2 Bear left on Route 237 for 2.4 miles to the end (Route 25), at a large traffic island.

38.6 Right for 1.5 miles to the Park and Ride lot on the right.

Final mileage: 40.1

Bicycle Repair Services

Ernie's Cycle Shop, 105 Conant Street, Westbrook (854-4090)

The Spokesperson, Springvale Commons, Springvale (324-5426)

Seger's Cycle, 865 Bridgton Road, Westbrook (854-5108)

20.

Western Lakes and Mountains Tour

Distance: 194 miles in four days: 40 miles the first day, 46 the second, 55 the third, and 53 the fourth.

Terrain: Generally rolling, with about ten long, steep hills. This is a fairly challenging tour.

Special features: Gracious New England towns, spectacular mountain and lake views, upper Androscoggin River, gorges and waterfalls, Rangeley Lake, Wilhelm Reich Museum, mineral museum.

Accommodations: Night before the tour, in Waterford (recommended start): *Kedarburn Inn* (583-6182). *Lake House Inn* (583-4182).

Alternative start: *Goodwin's Motor Inn*, South Paris (743-5121).

First and third nights: *Linnell Motel*, Rumford (the most convenient, 364-4511). *Madison Motor Inn*, Rumford (364-7973). *Blue Iris Motor Inn*, Rumford (364-4495).

Second Night: *Rangeley Inn*, Rangeley (864-3341). *Northwoods Bed and Breakfast*, Rangeley (864-2440). *Farmhouse Inn*, Rangeley (864-5805).

West-central Maine, stretching between Sebago and Rangeley Lakes near the New Hampshire border, is a region dotted with classic New England towns, rugged mountains and soft green hills, pristine lakes, and swift streams. Bicycling in the region is challenging, but you'll be amply rewarded by sweeping views, soaring downhill runs, and quite possibly the thrill of a deer poised at the edge of a field or a hawk nose-diving through the sky. There are many fewer tourists here than along the coast, and they are mostly hikers and fishing enthusiasts instead of beachgoers and boutique browsers. Traffic is light to moderate, even on the numbered roads, and nearly nonexistent on the unnumbered byways.

The tour starts from the village of Waterford, a New England jewel, which is a National Historic District. Large white houses with dark green shutters and a stately church cluster around the small green. Three of the houses are country inns—intimate affairs with a warm and cozy atmosphere and home-cooked meals. If you've never experienced the charm of an old-fashioned inn, here is a good excuse to do so.

From Waterford, the route heads north for about 18 miles to Bethel, going up and down hills with spectacular views of the neighboring hills and mountains. This type of scenery will repeat itself many times during the tour. The land is partly forested and partly farmed, with rough-hewn barns and big wooden farmhouses.

Bethel is another classic New England town, larger than Waterford, with fine old homes gracing its tree-shaded streets. Across from the green is the elegant Bethel Inn, a golden, 65-room landmark. Just down the street is the center of town, with wooden Victorian commercial buildings, and the handsome campus of Gould Academy, a preparatory school. As you glance across the green or the broad lawns of the campus, mountains pierce the horizon in all directions.

The 20-mile stretch from Bethel to Rumford is the easiest part of the tour, hugging the Androscoggin River. The river is calm here, held back by the dam in Rumford, as it curves gracefully between wooded hills and narrow farms along its banks.

Rumford is a small manufacturing city which lacks most of the charm and fine architecture found in so many other Maine communities. The massive Boise-Cascade paper mill dominates the town and its odor fills the nostrils. Fortunately, Rumford is compact, and as soon as you leave Route 2 you get back into the countryside.

Most of the 35-mile section from Rumford north to Rangeley Lake follows the Swift River, a small stream hemmed in by a narrow wooded valley. The population density drops dramatically; only an occasional house and the two tiny hamlets of Roxbury and Byron break the isolation until the cabins and cottages along the lake. In Byron is Coos Canyon, a narrow gorge through which the river surges forcefully. Beyond Byron the road climbs steadily to the crest of the divide between the Androscoggin River and the lakes to the north. From the divide, called Height of Land, an inspiring view unfolds across Mooselookmeguntic Lake to the White Mountains and Canada. A thrilling descent brings you to Rangeley Lake.

The Rangeley Lake region has long been a favorite for hikers, hunters, fishermen, and families spending their vacation in lakeside cottages. Visually, the lake is striking; it's fairly large (about seven miles long) and ringed by mountains. The town of Rangeley is attractively located on a small cove. Next to the center of town is the gracious yet reasonably priced Rangeley Inn.

After climbing out of town, you'll enjoy a long, gentle descent along the Sandy River. Like the Swift River, it flows through a narrow, nearly uninhabited valley. You'll pass Smalls Falls, a series of four cascades in quick succession, plummeting through a pine-rimmed gorge. Ahead lies the antique village of Weld, with a charming old general store and the turn-of-the-century Weld Inn standing guard above Webb (not Weld) Lake.

From Weld, 14 miles of gentle downhill grade bring you back to the Androscoggin River. You'll follow it on the opposite bank and then weave your way on back roads through the cluster of ponds that dot the landscape just east of Bethel. The West Paris area is rich in minerals and dotted with abandoned mines and quarries. A fascinating landmark is

Perham's Maine Mineral Store, which is not only a store, but also a museum displaying every mineral to be found in Maine and a scale model of a working feldspar quarry. Some of the minerals are displayed in ultraviolet light to best bring out their fluorescent colors and internal structure.

South of West Paris is Paris Hill, which is the finest traditional New England village that I've encountered in Maine, and one that is nearly undiscovered. The large, semicircular green crowns a high ridge with magnificent views of the rugged mountains to the west. Fronting on the green are elegant white houses with dark shutters and fanlights above the doors and an exceptionally elegant church. The route descends into the twin towns of South Paris and Norway, which form the commercial center for an extensive rural area between Lewiston and North Conway, New Hampshire. At South Paris, the route turns west for about 13 miles back to Waterford through a mostly wooded landscape dotted with ponds.

Directions for the ride

First day: Waterford to Rumford (40 miles)

Start from the junction of Routes 35 and 37 in Waterford (the inns cluster around this intersection). Waterford is about 50 miles northwest of Portland.

An alternative starting point is Goodwin's Motor Inn, on Routes 26 and 117 in South Paris. If you start here (which adds 12 miles to the first day, and subtracts it from the last day), turn right (west) from the motor inn onto Route 117 and follow it for about 3 miles to the intersection where Route 117 turns left and Route 118 goes straight. Go straight for 5.8 miles to Route 37 on the left. Turn left for 3 miles to Route 35 in Waterford, and turn right.

0.0   Head north out of Waterford on Route 35 for 4.6 miles to the end (merge left at the stop sign at the bottom of a long hill), in North Waterford.

Caution here. There's a steady climb out of Waterford with a good view from the top across fields stretching to forested hillsides, followed by a long, fast descent into North Waterford.

4.6   Bear left at the stop sign (still Route 35) for 1.1 miles to the intersection where Route 35 turns right and Route 5 South goes straight.

At the intersection, on the right, is an often-photographed sign indicating the direction and distance to nine Maine towns with the names of foreign countries and cities. The sign is aimed at traffic coming the other way, so you'll have to look back to see it.

5.7   Right on Route 35 (also Route 5 North) for 6.4 miles to the point where Route 35 turns right and Route 5 goes straight.

12.1   Straight for 6 miles to a crossroads where Route 5 turns right, toward Bethel.

The road goes along Songo Pond, lined with rustic, tree-shaded cottages.

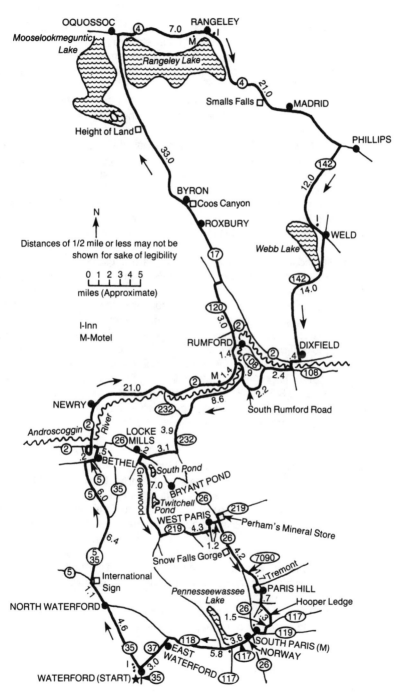

18.1 Turn right (still Route 5) for 0.2 mile to the Bethel town green, at the top of the steep hill. Route 5 curves 90 degrees left here.

On your right is the elegant Bethel Inn. Also fronting on the green is the Moses Mason House at 15 Broad Street, a stately Federal-era mansion built in 1813.

18.3 At the green, continue on Route 5 for ½ mile to the end (Route 26).

You'll go past the center of town on the right and then by the handsome red brick buildings of Gould Academy. It's worth spending some time in Bethel to stroll past the fine old houses along the green and the Victorian commercial buildings in town. There are several restaurants in town, and if you'd like a touch of class, the Bethel Inn serves excellent meals.

18.8 Turn left on Route 26 (also Route 5). After 0.1 mile, Routes 26 and 5 bear to the left. Bear left for 100 yards to the end, at the stop sign.

18.9 Left for another 100 yards to the intersection where Routes 2 East, 5 North, and 26 North bear left.

19.0 Bear left, and follow the main road, Route 2 East, for about 21 miles to the Linnell Motel on the left, on the outskirts of Rumford. (You'll come to the other motels first.)

Route 2 is fairly busy, but there's a good shoulder for most of this section. This is a flat ride along the Androscoggin River, with farmland along its banks and views of the mountains in the distance. If you're a geology buff, the gem and mineral store on the right at the beginning of this section is fascinating. Final mileage: 40.0.

Side Trip: After about 3 miles, if you bear left on a side road toward the Sunday River Ski Area for about 4 miles you'll come to the Artist's Bridge, an unusually picturesque covered bridge, built in 1872, that spans the Sunday River.

Second Day: Rumford to Rangeley (46 miles)

0.0 Go east toward Rumford on Route 2 for 2.8 miles (from the Linnell Motel) to the traffic light where Route 2 turns right and Route 120 goes straight.

Route 2 makes several turns in Rumford, but fortunately they are well marked. The road stays on the north bank of the river; if you cross it you've gone off the route. As you start down the long hill into Rumford, you have a dramatic view of the city, river, arched bridge, and mountain backdrop. Eat a hearty breakfast in Rumford and carry some extra food and liquids, as there is only one small store between here and Rangeley Lake.

2.8 Straight on Route 120 for 3 miles to an unmarked road on the right.

The land becomes pastoral shortly after you get onto Route 120. The Swift River is on your right.

5.8 Right across the bridge for 0.1 mile to the end (Route 17).

5.9 Left for about 33 miles to the end (Route 4).

The first half of this long section is gently rolling, following the Swift River upstream as it cascades alongside the road. There's a country store after about 7 miles in the hamlet of Roxbury. In Byron, 4 miles ahead, the river roars through Coos Canyon, a deep gorge where gold has been found. The picnic area is a great spot for a rest.

After the road diverges from the river, there's a steady climb for 2 miles to Beaver Pond, and some sharp ups and downs for the next 3 miles to the highest point, called Height of Land, which has an elevation of 2400 feet. To the left is a spectacular view of Mooselookmeguntic Lake and the northern White Mountains.

From here it's all downhill to Rangeley Lake, which you'll follow for the last few miles. **Caution:** The first 2 miles of the descent are

The International Sign in Lynchville is a landmark in western Maine.

very bumpy; then the road smooths out. At the end, in the village of Oquossoc, a grocery and restaurant are on the left.

39.0   Right on Route 4 for 7 miles into Rangeley.

You'll have two steep hills about ½ mile long on this stretch. Panoramic views of the lake and of distant mountains unfold across broad, sloping fields. Some of the peaks are over 4,000 feet high.

After about 3 miles, a dirt road on the left leads 0.8 mile uphill to one of Maine's more unusual attractions, the Wilhelm Reich Museum. Reich was a psychoanalyst and natural scientist with controversial theories of physical, biological, and sexual energy. He died in 1957 in prison, having been convicted of fraud for selling boxes in which one would sit to absorb the energy, which Reich called orgone. He is buried on the property.

In Rangeley, the Town and Lake Motel is on the right just before the town. The Rangeley Inn, a Victorian classic, is on the left just beyond the center of town. The Farmhouse Inn is a mile past town. There are several restaurants in town. One of them, Doc Grant's, has a sign in front saying that Rangeley is halfway between the North Pole and the Equator.

Final mileage: 46.0.

Third Day: Rangeley-Weld-Rumford (55 miles)

0.0   From Rangeley, continue on Route 4 for about 21 miles to Route 142 on the right.

Be sure to eat a hearty breakfast in Rangeley and stock up on food, as there is no food until Weld, 33 miles away. There are a couple of steep hills to get out of Rangeley; then it's mostly downhill as you follow the Sandy River downstream.

About 12 miles out of town, Smalls Falls will be on your right, at a rest area. It's a spectacular chain of four waterfalls in quick succession that plunge through a pine-fringed gorge. A trail leads for about 200 yards to Chandlers Mill Stream Falls, which is also worth seeing.

21.0   Right on Route 142 for about 12 miles to the crossroads where Route 142 turns right, in Weld.

This is the most difficult section of the tour, with several long, steep hills. Shortly before Weld you'll go along Webb Lake. The Weld Inn, across the road from the lake, is a good spot for lunch. There's also a country store at the crossroads.

33.0   Right on Route 142 for about 14 miles to the end (Route 2), in Dixfield.

Most of this section is a gentle downhill grade, following the Webb River. There's a food store just before the end.

47.0   Right on Route 2 for 0.4 mile to the first left (the sign says "to Peru").

47.4 Left, crossing the Androscoggin River, for 0.3 mile to the crossroads (Route 108) and stop sign.

47.7 Right on Route 108 for 2.4 miles to the first road (unmarked) bearing left.

50.1 Bear left. After 2.2 miles you will merge head-on at a "Yield" sign into a larger road. Continue straight for 0.9 mile to the end (Route 2).

53.2 Left for 1.4 miles to the Linnell Motel on the right. The other motels are farther along Route 2.
Final mileage: 54.6

Fourth Day: Rumford-South Paris-Waterford (53 miles)

0.0 Go east toward Rumford on Route 2 for 1.4 miles (from the Linnell Motel) to South Rumford Road on the right (a sign says "to South Rumford").

1.4 Right for 0.9 mile to a fork where the main road curves right and a smaller road goes straight.

2.3 Curve right on the main road for 8.6 miles to the end (Route 232), at a stop sign and grassy traffic island.
This is a lovely run along the Androscoggin River.

10.9 Bear left on Route 232 for 3.9 miles to the first paved right.
There is a red brick house on the far corner.

14.8 Right for 3.1 miles to the end (merge right on Route 26).
The narrow road winds along the shore of North Pond.

17.9 Bear right on Route 26 for 0.2 mile to the first left (a sign says "to Mount Abram Ski Area").
You'll pass a restaurant on the left.

18.1 Left for 100 yards to Greenwood Road on the left, immediately after the railroad tracks.

18.2 Turn 90 degrees left on Greenwood Road (don't bear left uphill on Knoll Road) for 7 miles to Route 219 on the left (a sign says "to West Paris"). At the beginning of this stretch you'll hug the shore of unspoiled South Pond; just ahead you'll ride alongside Twitchell Pond.

25.2 Turn left on Route 219 for 4.3 miles to the end (Route 219 turns left).
Two smaller roads bear off to the right on this section, but stay on the main road. This is a relaxing ride, mostly a gentle descent, along the Little Androscoggin River.

29.5 Left at the end (still Route 219) for 1.2 miles to the end (Route 26).
You will go through West Paris, a town with fine rambling houses and a big yellow schoolhouse. At the end, Perham's Maine Mineral Store, a landmark since 1919, is 100 yards to the left. Across the road is a general store where you can buy food.

30.7 Right on Route 26 (if you visited Perham's, turn left when you leave) for 4.2 miles to Fire Road 7090 (marked by a small green sign), which bears left. It's shortly after a crossroads.

After 2.2 miles, you will pass Snow Falls Gorge on the right. Here the Little Androscoggin River sluices through narrow passages between boulders. It's a great picnic spot.

34.9 Bear left on Fire Road 7090 for 1.7 miles to a crossroads (Tremont Street), in Paris Hill.

The road climbs steeply, but you will be rewarded with a sweeping view and a long, fast descent.

36.6 Right at the crossroads for 0.2 mile to the end, which is the same road you were on before the crossroads.

Paris Hill is a classic, elegant New England village. When you ride behind the church, you will pass the pillared Hannibal Hamlin House (a private residence) perched on the brow of the hill on the right. Hamlin was Vice-President under Abraham Lincoln. Next to it is the Paris Hill Museum and Library, a square, granite building that looks more like a jail, and, indeed, it was the Oxford County Jail from 1822 to 1896. From behind the museum, an inspiring view extends west to the White Mountains.

36.8 Turn right at the end. Just ahead is a fork. Bear slightly left on the main road for 0.7 mile to another fork, at a five-way intersection.

37.5 Bear slightly left again on Hooper Ledge Road (don't turn almost 90 degrees left) for 1.3 miles to the end (merge right on Route 117 at the bottom of the hill; **caution** here).

This is a wonderful downhill ride with some fine views.

38.8 Bear right on Route 117, and follow it for 5.1 miles to the intersection where Route 117 turns left and Route 118 goes straight, opposite Pennesseewassee Lake on the right.

Route 117 turns several times as it threads through the twin towns of South Paris and Norway, but it is well marked. As you come into South Paris, notice the dam on the right as you cross the Little Androscoggin River. If you started from Goodwin's Motor Inn, it's on the right after about 2 miles.

43.9 Straight on Route 118 for 5.8 miles to Route 37 on the left, in East Waterford.

There's a restaurant on the right shortly before the intersection.

49.7 Turn left on Route 37 for 3 miles to the end (Route 35), back in Waterford.

You'll pass a wonderful old general store on the right after ½ mile. Just before the end, you'll go along wooded Keoka Lake on the left. Final mileage: 52.7.

Bicycle Repair Services

Wallace's Wheels, 703 Crescent Avenue, Rumford (364-7946)

21.

Androscoggin Valley Tour: Lewiston—Auburn—Turner—Greene

Distance: 35 miles
Terrain: Gently rolling, with one long, steep hill and a few short ones.
Special features: Bates College, Lake Auburn, ridge with spectacular views, lovely rolling countryside.

Just north of the twin cities of Lewiston and Auburn lies a rural area, bisected by the Androscoggin River, that provides some superb cycling. The region's most attractive feature is its tranquillity—it is virtually unvisited by tourists and not on the way to any center of population. This means that the secondary roads are nearly traffic free.

The ride starts from Bates College, which is located on the northern edge of Lewiston. The twin cities, with a combined population of about 65,000, form the second largest metropolitan area in the state. The powerful falls on the Androscoggin, which flows between the two communities, sparked the development of shoe and textile manufacturing during the 1830s. These two industries still form an important part of the area's economy. The tour stays north of the downtown and manufacturing areas—which are not very pleasant to bicycle through—and instead heads quickly into the countryside.

Bates College (the author's alma mater, '69) is a small, academically rigorous liberal arts institution with a well-manicured campus shaded by towering elms. The centerpiece of the campus is Hathorn Hall, a handsome brick building with a bell tower. Built in 1856, it is the original academic building of the college and is listed on the National Register of Historic Places. Opposite the campus, on the corner of College Street and Mountain Avenue, is Mount David, a rocky hill from which there's a fine view of the college and the city of Lewiston. Dominating the skyline is Saints Peter and Paul Church, which looks like a cathedral and can hold 2,000 worshippers.

From Bates, the ride heads west across the new bridge over the Androscoggin River into Auburn. The bridge is only a half mile from the campus. Once in Auburn, you'll quickly enter rural countryside. The route skirts most of Lake Auburn, which is the water supply for the twin cities and nearly undeveloped. Quiet secondary roads lead through gently rolling farmland which slopes down to the lake about a quarter mile away.

You'll ride through West Auburn, an unspoiled New England village with a few fine old houses and a small church. Beyond, the route descends steeply to the lake and hugs its shore.

North of Lake Auburn, you'll climb onto a magnificent open ridge with panoramic views of the hills and mountains of western Maine. While cycling along the ridge, you'll see horses and cows grazing contentedly on broad expanses of pasture. At the northernmost point of the route, you'll descend into the valley of the Androscoggin and cross the river to the eastern bank. The route turns south, following the river past farmland, and then curving inland through forest.

After a few miles you'll pedal through Greene, another attractive little town with a Gothic-style church and a fine old grange hall. From Greene, you'll return to the campus along College Road, a pleasant secondary road that passes through gently rolling farmland.

Directions for the ride

Start from Bates College, which is a mile north of downtown Lewiston and just east of Route 202.

From the Maine Turnpike, take the Lewiston exit (exit 13). Merge right at the end of the ramp onto Route 196. Go 1.2 miles to East Avenue on the right, at a traffic light (signs say "to Winthrop" and "to Bates College"). Turn right for 0.9 mile to Webster Street, at the second traffic light. Turn left for 0.8 mile to College Street, which crosses Webster Street at the third traffic light. Turn right for ½ mile to the campus on your right. Park where legal on College Street or on Mountain Avenue, which is on the left opposite the campus.

The college snack bar, called the Den, is an inexpensive place to eat before or after the ride. It's in the student union building, Chase Hall, which is on Campus Avenue, the street bordering the campus on the south. (College Street borders the campus on the west.)

Hathorn Hall, built in 1856, graces the elm-shaped campus of Bates College.

0.0 Head north on College Street, with the campus on your right, for 0.2 mile to Russell Street, at the traffic light.

0.2 Left for 0.3 mile to Route 202, at the traffic light.

0.5 Straight for 1.1 mile to Route 4, at the next traffic light.

It's at the far end of the bridge across the Androscoggin River.

1.6 Straight onto Mount Auburn Avenue for 0.4 mile to a crossroads (Turner Street) and stop sign.

You go past Auburn Mall, the area's largest, on the right.

2.0 Straight for 1.1 miles to the end, at the "Yield" sign (merge right on Summer Street).

The road passes through farmland, with Lake Auburn in the distance on the right.

3.1 Bear right on Summer Street for 0.7 mile to a fork (Summer Street bears right).

3.8 Bear right for 0.4 mile to the end, at the "Yield" sign (merge right).

4.2 Bear right for 3.3 miles to Lake Shore Drive on the right, just past the bottom of the big hill. A grocery is on the left at the intersection.

On this stretch are two forks where a smaller road bears right and then left, but stay on the main road. This is a lovely ride through rolling farmland, passing rambling old farmhouses. You'll climb gradually to

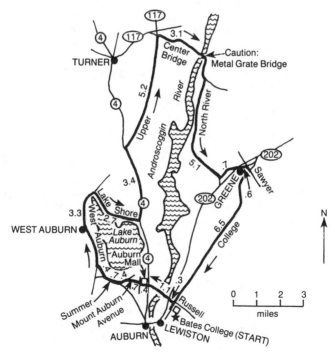

25 Bicycle Tours in Maine © 1986 Backcountry Publications

West Auburn; then a flying downhill run brings you to the shore of Lake Auburn.

7.5   Right on Lake Shore Drive for 2.7 miles to the end (Route 4).

The road hugs the lakeshore, passing a snack bar on the right about halfway along.

10.2   Left on Route 4 for 3.4 miles to an unmarked road that bears right uphill immediately after a True Value hardware store on the right.

There's a concrete traffic island in the intersection. Route 4 is heavily traveled, but it has a wide shoulder.

13.6   Bear right for 5.2 miles to the crossroads at the bottom of the steep hill, just before Cobb Road on the right.

Caution: The crossroads comes up suddenly, while you are descending a steep grade. The road climbs steadily, with one very steep section, onto a high ridge with splendid views. You'll pass rambling old farmhouses attached to their barns, a hallmark of rural Maine architecture.

18.8   Turn right at the crossroads (**Caution:** It's a fairly sharp right). Go 3.1 miles to a fork where a smaller road bears right, about a mile after the metal-grate bridge across the Androscoggin.

Caution: The metal grating is very slippery when wet; there's a very real danger of falling and hurting yourself. If the road is wet, or even if the metal may be wet from condensation, please walk across.

21.9   Bear right on the smaller road for 5.1 miles to the end.

This is another lovely back road, passing farms with views of the river in the distance.

27.0   Left for 0.3 mile to a fork where the main road bears right.

Just after you turn left, the back of an IGA supermarket, a corrugated metal building, is on the right.

27.3   Bear right for 0.4 mile to a diagonal crossroads (Route 202).

27.7   Cross Route 202 diagonally onto Main Street (**Caution** here). Go 0.6 mile to a crossroads (Sawyer Road on the right).

You'll go through Greene. Notice the Gothic-style church, grange hall, and little library.

28.3   Right on Sawyer Road for 0.1 mile to the crossroads (College Road).

28.4   Right for 6.7 miles to Bates College on the left, just after the traffic light.

There are several short hills on this stretch. You'll pass a small grocery on the right after about 4 miles.

Final mileage: 35.1.

Bicycle Repair Services

Moe's Bicycle Shop, 54 Sabattus Street, Lewiston (783-2641)
Twin City Cyclery, 199 Bartlett Street, Lewiston (783-0622)
Roy's Bicycle Shop, 51 Farwell Street, Lewiston (783-9090)
Rainbow Bicycle Center, 1225 Center Street, Auburn (784-7576)

22.

Lakes of Central Maine: Augusta— Hallowell—Litchfield—Winthrop

Distance: 38 miles
Terrain: Rolling, with a few steep hills.
Special features: Antique shops and fine architecture in Hallowell, lakeshore scenery, side trip to Monmouth Museum (open 1-4 p.m.).

The region just west of Augusta, dominated by a cluster of lakes, is ideal for bicycling. A network of lightly-traveled back roads leads along and between the lakes, passing through rolling farmland and rustic small towns.

The ride starts from the western edge of Augusta, a compact city, sloping gradually along both banks of the Kennebec River. After two and a half miles, the route plunges steeply down to Hallowell, a riverfront town which abounds in 19th-century architecture and is a center for antique dealers. From Hallowell, the road climbs more gradually out of the Kennebec Valley, and heads through farms and woodlots to Cobbossee-contee Lake (usually shortened to Cobbossee), the largest of the three lakes you'll see on the ride.

After going along Cobbossee, it's not far to Lake Annabessacook. The ride curves north along the lakeshore and heads into Winthrop, a scenic town sandwiched between Lake Annabessacook on the south and Maranacook Lake on the north. Leaving Winthrop, you'll hug the shore of Maranacook Lake for several miles before turning east back to Augusta. The last section of the tour leads primarily through open farming country, ascending onto several ridges with fine views.

Augusta itself is worth a visit after the ride. The granite-domed State House, designed by Charles Bulfinch, is easily the most impressive building in town. It is located just south of Route 202, near the river on the west bank. Adjacent to the State House is the Maine State Museum, with an outstanding collection of exhibits relating to Maine's history, industry, and cultural life. Across the street from the State House is the elegant Blaine House, originally built for a sea captain and now the Governor's residence. Tours are offered on weekday afternoons. On the east bank of the Kennebec, just north of Route 202, is a restoration of Fort Western, a trading post built in 1754 for protection from hostile Indians.

Directions for the ride

Start from Sears, Turnpike Mall, Augusta. It's on Route 202, just west of the Maine Turnpike and Route 95.

0.0   Right out of the east side of the parking lot, paralleling the Maine Turnpike on your left. (Don't get on Route 202.) Go 1.3 miles to the end.

1.3   Left for 1.3 miles to the end (Route 201), in Hallowell.

Caution: There is a long, steep downhill into Hallowell—take it easy. The town, on the Kennebec River about 2 miles south of Augusta, boasts some superb 19th-century commercial and domestic architecture and is worth exploring. The downtown area consists of three- and four-story brick buildings, constructed during the late 1800s, which face each other across Route 201. The three streets closest to Route 201 and running parallel with it (on your right as you're heading down the hill into town), are lined with fine Victorian, Federal-era and Georgian houses. Just before the bottom of the hill, notice the handsome yellow brick town hall, built in 1898, on your left. You'll also pass the Maine Publicity Bureau, which operates the visitor center at the southern end of the Maine Turnpike.

2.6   Right at the bottom of the hill on Route 201 (Water Street) for 0.2 mile to Temple Street on the right. It runs one short block to a stone church.

You'll go through downtown Hallowell, passing a cluster of antique shops and restaurants.

2.8   Right on Temple Street for one block to the end (Second Street).

2.9   Left for ¼ mile to a fork where Vaughn Street bears left and the main road goes straight.

Caution: There are treacherous diagonal railroad tracks shortly after you turn left. Please dismount.

3.1   Continue straight on the main road for 1 mile to a crossroads, shortly after the bridge over the Maine Turnpike.

This is a steady but moderate climb away from the river, not nearly as steep as the descent into Hallowell.

4.1   Right for 1.3 miles to Outlet Road, which bears left uphill. The main road curves 90 degrees left after 0.2 mile.

5.4   Bear left for 3.5 miles to the end.

This is a lovely back road through mostly wooded landscape, passing some rambling farmhouses. Jimmie Pond will be on your right after 2 miles, nestled in the woods. At the end, Cobbosseecontee Lake is in front of you.

8.9   Left for 5 miles to the end (merge to the right at a stop sign).

The road parallels the lake about ½ mile from its shore, winding past woods and small farms. Only a few dirt roads lead to the lake, which is pleasantly undeveloped.

13.9   Bear right for 0.1 mile to the fork, in the village of Litchfield (also called Purgatory Village).

Notice the small dam on your left. Litchfield is a tiny community with just a few houses and no store.

14.0   Bear right, and immediately bear right again at another fork, uphill. Go 3 miles to a crossroads.

Caution: There is a steep, bumpy downhill after 2 miles. This is the most difficult section of the ride, with several short steep hills and one long one. After 2 miles, the road descends steeply to the southern end of Cobbosseecontee Lake, where you'll have a nice view. At the top of each hill, look back for additional good views.

17.0   Right at the crossroads for 1.8 miles to the end (Route 135).

The road runs parallel to a stream that flows between Lake Annabessacook and Cobbosseecontee. Notice the little dam on your right just before the end.

18.8   Left on Route 135 for 0.6 mile to a smaller road that bears right.

Side Trip: Here the ride bears right, but if you continue straight for 2.6 miles to Route 132, at the end, you'll see the Monmouth Museum on the left. This is a living history museum of rural life in Maine during

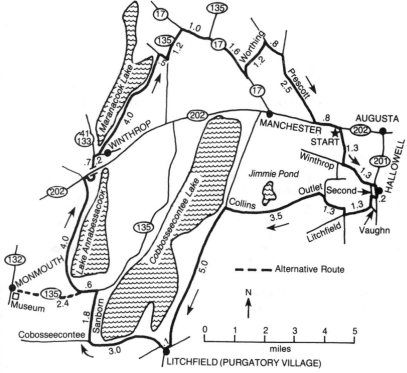

25 Bicycle Tours in Maine © 1986 Backcountry Publications

the 19th century, including a blacksmith shop, country store, house with period furnishings, and other buildings.

19.4   Bear right on the smaller road (turn sharp left if you're coming from the museum) for 4 miles to a crossroads (Route 202) and stop sign.

This is an inspiring stretch along Lake Annabessacook, rolling through prosperous farms with views of the lake in the distance across the fields. When you come to Route 202, there are grocery stores at the intersection. Notice the fine Victorian house on the far side of the intersection.

23.4   Right on Route 202 for 100 yards to Routes 41 and 133, which bear right.

23.5   Bear right for 0.7 mile to Main Street, which bears right (a sign says "to Winthrop").

24.2   Bear right for 0.2 mile to Bowdoin Street on the left just before the center of town. It's your first left.

There's a restaurant and grocery in Winthrop.

24.4   Left for 4 miles to the end, at a T-intersection and stop sign.

This is a lovely ride hugging the shore of Maranacook Lake, passing cozy cottages nestled in the woods on the lakefront.

28.4   Right for ½ mile to the end (Route 135).

28.9   Left for 1.2 miles to the end (Route 17).

30.1   Turn right. After 1 mile, Route 135 turns left, but continue straight for 1.6 miles to Worthing Road on left. It's a sharp left that comes up while you're going downhill.

After turning right on Route 17, you'll climb a long, steady hill with a church on top. As you're climbing, look back for a spectacular view across sweeping farmland. On the far side of the hill, you can see Cobbosseecontee Lake on your right, in the distance across broad fields.

32.7   Sharp left on Worthing Road for 1.2 miles to the end.

33.9   Right for 0.8 mile to the end (Prescott Road).

You'll pass a small isolated meetinghouse on the left, dating from 1795, followed by an exhilarating downhill run.

34.7   Right on Prescott Road for 2.5 miles to the end (merge left on Route 202). The road passes through large farms and ascends onto a hillside with inspiring views.

37.2   Bear left on Route 202 for 0.8 mile to Turnpike Mall on the right. Final mileage: 38.0

Bicycle Repair Services

Auclair's Cycle Shop, 64 Bangor Street, Augusta (623-4351)
Poulin Cycle, 558 Riverside Drive, Augusta (623-1166)

23.

Bangor—Hermon—Levant

Distance: 26 miles
Terrain: Pleasantly rolling, with a few moderate hills.
Special features: Prosperous farming country, ridges with good views.
Road surface: 1.2 miles of hard-packed dirt road.

The best bicycling in the Bangor area is west of the city. To the north and east are relatively few paved roads, and most of these go through miles of woodland without much variation in the scenery. To the south, a loop ride will inevitably involve pedaling on Route 1A or 15, both of which are heavily traveled and not particularly attractive. To the west, fortunately, lies rolling open farm country and quiet villages linked by a network of back roads with very little traffic.

The ride starts from the western edge of Bangor, across from Maine's largest airport. With a population of about 32,000, it is the only real city in the northern two-thirds of the state. The next largest community to the north, Presque Isle (population 12,000), is 150 miles away. Heading west from Bangor, the route immediately heads into open farm country traversed by low ridges. Most of the landscape has a prosperous, well-trimmed appearance, with rambling farmhouses, big barns, and woodpiles neatly stacked beside them. Many of the pastures are home to horses and cattle that graze contentedly. Following the style unique to northern New England, many of the houses and barns are connected into one elongated habitat.

Most of the westward leg of the ride passes through Hermon, a farming community which has not been despoiled by suburban development. The village center lies a mile south of the route. After about 10 miles, the route turns north along a ridge between two small streams. You'll dip into a valley and then climb gradually along a smooth dirt road to the summit of another ridge, where a sweeping view and a glorious downhill run will reward your efforts. At the bottom lies Levant, another undeveloped farming village, which borders Bangor on the northwest. The country store here is a good spot for a breather. The homestretch, from Levant back to Bangor, continues through gently rolling farmland with some extensive views.

Directions for the ride
Start from Airport Mall in Bangor. It is on Route 222 (Union Street), a mile

west of Route 95. If you're coming from the south, follow Route 95 to exit 47 (a sign says "to Route 222 and Airport"). At the end of the ramp is Ohio Street, which parallels Route 222 ¼ mile north of it. Turn left on Ohio Street and then left again, following the signs to Route 222. When you come to Route 222, turn right (west) for one mile to the mall, which will be on your right. If you're coming from the north, exit from Route 95 directly onto Route 222. Turn right (west) for one mile to the mall on your right.

0.0 Turn right (west) on Route 222. Just ahead is a traffic light. Continue on Route 222 for 3 miles to Billings Road on the left, as you start to go uphill.

3.1 Left for 1.9 miles to the second crossroads, Fuller Road.

There is a gradual climb onto a ridge with panoramic views to your left, followed by a swooping descent.

5.0 Right on Fuller Road for 5.5 miles to a crossroads and stop sign.

The road passes through a harmonious mix of woods and farmland, up and over a few small hills.

10.5 Right at the crossroads for 2.3 miles to a fork.

The road traverses a low ridge with rolling farmland on both sides. Just before the fork, a small white church will be on your left.

12.8 Bear right at fork. After 1.7 miles, a dirt road, Quinn Road, bears left. Continue on the paved road for 0.2 mile to another dirt road that bears left. The ride bears left here.

This road is hard-packed and you should have no trouble bicycling on it. If you prefer to avoid it (you'll miss a great downhill run and a

Bicycling is a pleasure on the lightly-traveled backroads west of Bangor.

spectacular view if you do), continue on the paved road for 1.5 miles to the end (Route 222), turn right for 0.9 mile to the crossroads in the village of Levant, and resume at mile **18.0.**

14.7   Bear left on the dirt road (Pember Road, unmarked) for 1.2 miles to Route 222, at the stop sign.

The road climbs gradually through farmland onto a ridge. While researching the ride, I spotted a deer bounding across the road.

15.9   Right on Route 222 for 2.1 miles to a crossroads in the village of Levant.

There's a country store on the left at the intersection. Enjoy the long, steady descent from the ridge, and the magnificent view unfolding before you as you start to go down. **Caution:** Watch for occasional bumps and potholes during the descent.

18.0   Left at the crossroads for 0.3 mile to Phillips Road, which bears right.

18.3   Bear right. After 2.5 miles the main road curves sharply right. Continue 5.1 miles to a traffic light (Griffin Road on the right).

There's a convenience store on the far left corner. Phillips Road becomes Ohio Street. If you look to your left at the traffic light, you'll see a steel-trussed bridge, called the Bullseye Bridge, over the Kenduskeag Stream. This river joins the Penobscot River in downtown Bangor.

25.9   Right at the traffic light for 0.3 mile to the mall on your left, just before Route 222.

Final mileage: 26.2

Bicycle Repair Services
Pat's Bike Shop, 373 Wilson Street, Brewer (989-2900)
Rose Bicycle, 36A Main Street, Orono (866-3525)
Main Street Mountain Bikes, 27 North Main Street, Old Town (827-0200)
Wilderness Sports, 33 School Street, Bangor (945-0966)

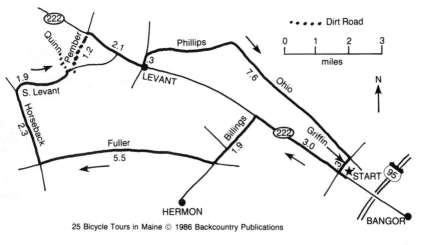

25 Bicycle Tours in Maine © 1986 Backcountry Publications

24.

The County: Touring the Top of Maine

Distance: 270 miles in 5 days: 41 the first day, 63 the second, 58 the third, 50 the fourth, and 58 the fifth.

Terrain: Hilly. This is a challenging tour.

Accommodations: At start: *Katahdin Valley Motel,* Sherman (356-4554).

First night: *Shiretown Motor Inn.* Houlton (532-9421), *Ivey's Motor Lodge,* Houlton (532-4206).

Second Night: *Days Inn,* Caribou (493-3311). *Daigle's Bed & Breakfast,* Caribou (498-2567). Less fancy. *Old Iron Inn,* Caribou (492-4766).

Third night: *Rock's Motel,* Fort Kent (834-3133). *Daigle's Bed & Breakfast,* Fort Kent (834-5803).

Fourth night: *Four Seasons Motel,* Ashland (435-8255).

Be sure to arrange your accommodations in advance.

Caution: This tour has some long, isolated stretches with no stores or restaurants. Be sure to carry extra food and water. Bring three waterbottles and keep them filled.

The last two days of the tour follow Route 11, which has heavy lumber truck traffic on weekdays. Try to finish the tour on a Saturday and Sunday.

Special features: Wide open potato country, covered bridge, unspoiled lakes, Saint John and Aroostook Rivers, Lumberman's Museum, views of Mount Katahdin.

Northern Maine has a landscape unlike anything else in New England. Its dominant feature is its expansiveness. Near the eastern border, vast treeless fields stretch to the horizon, sweeping up and over broad rolling hills. Further west, uninhabited forests extend for dozens of miles, traversed by only a few logging roads. Wild rivers and pristine lakes, undeveloped except for a few summer cottages (locally called "camps"), abound. Towns are small and, with the exception of the ones along Route 1, far apart. The largest town, Presque Isle, has only about 12,000 people.

Aroostook County is to Maine what Texas is to the United States, but with none of the Lone Star State's flash and swagger. Residents of Aroostook refer to it simply as "The County," implying that Maine's 15 other counties don't quite measure up; and in size, this is certainly true. Aroostook covers a fifth of Maine, an area the size of Rhode Island and Connecticut combined—but with one-fortieth of the population.

Another of the County's superlatives is the friendliness and honesty of the people. Aroostook is one of few places in the country where people frequently started conversations with me as if I were an old friend. In every town, the sight of my bicycle would prompt people to ask where I was headed and how long I'd been on the road, wish me good luck, and express the wish that they were doing the same thing. In Fort Kent, I paid for groceries with two ten-dollar bills stuck together. The clerk, not noticing this until after I'd left the store, chased me down the road to return one of the bills. When I asked a policeman in Houlton if cyclists could leave their cars at the police station, not only did he agree, but he also pointed out every back road in the area and interesting spots to see.

The County is host to several old-fashioned local festivals and agricultural fairs. The two largest are the Potato Blossom Festival, held in late July in Fort Fairfield (10 miles east of Presque Isle and Caribou), and the Northern Maine Fair, held in early August at the Presque Isle Fairgrounds. Keep in mind that if your tour coincides with a festival, accommodations will be difficult to find unless reserved far in advance.

The tour starts from Sherman, a small village in the southeastern corner of the County. Within a couple of miles, the route ascends onto a long, high ridge, the first of dozens that undulate across the landscape. From its flank, panoramic views unfold to the horizon across large farms. On a clear day you can see the distinctive hump of Mount Katahdin, the highest in Maine, about 25 miles away. As you approach Houlton, about 40 miles northeast of the start, you start to see potato farms that comprise most of the land in the eastern part of the County. Houlton is an attractive town of about 7,000 with a wide central square. A unique fountain, with a statue of a young boy holding a leaking boot, stands just east of town.

From Houlton, the tour heads north to Caribou through the heart of the potato-growing region. The potato barns, large buildings nearly buried by earth embankments to protect the harvest from the cold, are a distinctive feature of the landscape. The potatoes blossom in late July, covering the fields with a delicate carpet of pink and white flowers. In October, when the potatoes are harvested, the schools close so that the children can help. In Caribou, the second largest town in the County (population 10,000), the Nylander Museum is worth a visit. It has exhibits of local history, geology, vegetation, and Indian artifacts.

On the third day of the tour, you'll continue through the potato-growing region in a northwesterly direction to Fort Kent, on the New Brunswick border near Maine's northern tip. The route passes through New Sweden, a village where most of the residents are of Swedish descent—an ethnic oasis in a predominantly French-Canadian area. Ahead, the road follows the shore of two large, unspoiled lakes, Madawaska Lake and Long Lake, and descends to the banks of the Saint John River, which separates Maine from Canada at the top of the state. The last 12 miles hug the river into Fort Kent. Overlooking the river near the center of town is the Fort Kent Blockhouse, built in 1840 during the bloodless Aroostook War, a boundary dispute between New Brunswick and Maine's lumber interests.

From Fort Kent, the remainder of the tour heads due south through hilly countryside that becomes progressively more forested. The area and the vast expanses of woodland to the west are dominated by the lumber industry and a few scattered hunting and fishing camps. About 10 miles south of Fort Kent there's a lovely run alongside Eagle Lake. Beyond Ashland is a nearly unbroken 30-mile stretch of forest. In Patten, nine miles from the end of the tour, the Lumberman's Museum is one of the outstanding attractions of Northern Maine. Its nine buildings, crammed with tools and other artifacts, are an authentic restoration of a lumber camp, including the bunkhouse, cooking quarters, sawmill, and blacksmith shop. The last stretch from Patten to Sherman affords magnificent views of Mount Katahdin on the western horizon.

Directions for the ride:

First Day: Sherman to Houlton (41 miles)

Start from the Katahdin Valley Motel on Route 158 in Sherman, immediately west of Route 95. Sherman is about 80 miles north of Bangor. It's okay to leave your car here if you stay at the motel the night before your tour. The restaurant next to the motel is a logical spot for breakfast.

An alternative starting point is the police station in Houlton, on Route 2, ½ mile east of the center of town. If you start from here, turn right (east) on Route 2 for 0.4 mile to Foxcroft Road on the left, just as Route 2 starts to climb a long hill. Pick up the tour at mile **2.4** of the second day. Be sure to tell the police that you'll be leaving your car for several days.

0.0 Left (east) from the motel on Route 158 for 1.5 miles to a fork where Route 158 bears right and a smaller road bears left.

This is the village of Sherman Mills. Notice the fine church at the fork. Just before the fork is a wonderful Victorian house on the left, with an infinite number of gables.

1.5 Bear left at the fork for 5 miles to the end (merge head-on into Route 2).

The road climbs gradually onto a ridge with sweeping views across dairy farms. Look back over your left shoulder for a view of Mount Katahdin. You'll pass a couple of partially buried potato barns, the first of hundreds that are a hallmark of the potato-growing region.

6.5 Straight on Route 2 for about 7 miles to a crossroads where Route 2 turns right, in Island Falls.

13.5 Right (still Route 2) for about 7 miles to a road that bears right just before a railroad overpass (a sign says "to Oakfield").

Just after you turn, there's a bell tower on your left. It was originally on top of the high school, built in 1902. You'll pass Upper Mattawamkeag Lake on your right, across from the May Mountain ski area. May

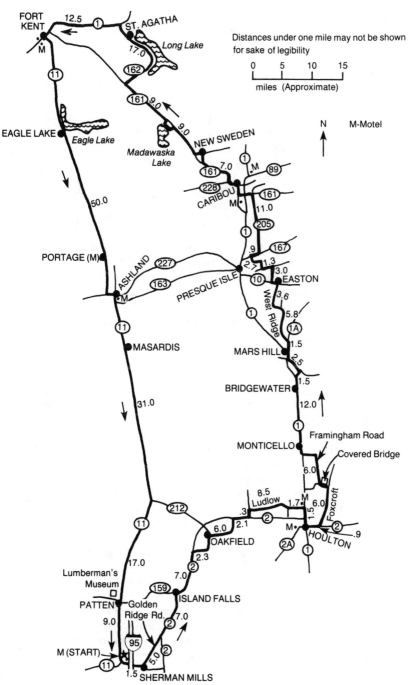

Distances under one mile may not be shown
for sake of legibility

0   5   10   15

miles (Approximate)

N   M-Motel

25 Bicycle Tours in Maine © 1986 Backcountry Publications

Mountain is really a round grassy hill.

20.5 Bear right for 2.3 miles to an unmarked road on the right, in the center of Oakfield.

22.8 Right for about 6 miles to the end (Route 2).

A grocery is on the left just after you turn right. There's a tough hill heading out of town. Beyond, the road winds through lovely rolling farmland with wooded hills in the distance, passing big old barns and farmhouses. **Caution:** Be careful when crossing the diagonal railroad tracks after about 4 miles. Please dismount.

28.8 Right on Route 2 for 2.1 miles to an unmarked road on the left, about a mile beyond Route 95.

There's a snack bar at the intersection with Route 95.

30.9 Left for 0.3 mile to the first right.

31.2 Right for about 8.5 miles to the intersection where the main road curves left and Mooers Road turns right.

The road traverses a long, open hillside with great views. **Caution:** Watch for occasional potholes at the beginning.

39.7 Curve left on the main road for 1.7 miles to the end (Route 1), on the outskirts of Houlton.

The Shiretown Motor Inn is on your left at the intersection, and Ivey's Motor Lodge is straight ahead on the other side of Route 1.

Final mileage: 41.4.

Second Day: Houlton to Caribou (63 miles)

0.0 Head south on Route 1 (toward the center of Houlton) for 1.5 miles to the end, where Routes 1 and 2 turn left (a sign says "Woodstock, Calais").

1.5 Left on Route 2 (also Military Street) for 0.9 mile to Foxcroft Road on the left, just as Route 2 starts to climb a long hill.

After you turn on Route 2, the center of town is one block to your left. Notice the solid rows of brick business buildings from the late 19th century on both sides of a wide square. You'll pass the leaking boot fountain on the left after 0.4 mile.

2.4 Left on Foxcroft Road for 6 miles to Framingham Road on the left, at the bottom of a steep little hill. A sign may say "Covered bridge".

8.4 Left for ½ mile to a fork where one road bears right and the other goes straight.

The road parallels the Littleton Bridge, Maine's newest covered bridge, built in 1911.

8.9 Bear right (still Framingham Road) for 6 miles to a crossroads and stop sign (Route 1).

After you bear right, the large round hill directly ahead of you in the distance is Mars Hill. You'll see it for the next 20 miles.

14.9 Right on Route 1 for about 12 miles to an unmarked road on the right, about 2 miles beyond Bridgewater (a sign says "to Centerville and

Florenceville, New Brunswick").

Route 1 is so straight that you can see it stretch ahead for miles as it goes up and down long, gradual hills. The towns of Monticello and Bridgewater are strung out along the highway with no real centers, but there are grocery stores and snack bars.

26.9 Continue on Route 1 for 0.2 mile to a road that bears right. (Don't turn right at the sign for Centerville and Florenceville, or you'll end up in Canada.)

27.1 Bear right for 1.5 miles to the end.

This road, and the next one, are narrow byways threading through potato farms.

28.6 Left for 2.5 miles to the diagonal crossroads (Route 1).

31.1 Bear right for 0.8 mile to the point where Route 1 turns left and Route 1A goes straight, in the town of Mars Hill.

The hill towers several hundred feet above the town. There's a food store and a snack bar here.

31.9 Straight on Route 1A for 0.7 mile to West Ridge Road, which bears left.

32.6 Bear left for 5.8 miles to a fork (Bangor Road bears right).

You'll pass a small airport as soon as you turn. Beyond, the road climbs onto a broad ridge with panoramic views across the wide open countryside.

38.4 Bear left at the fork for 3.6 miles to the end (Route 10), in the tiny hamlet of Easton.

There's an appealing country store here.

42.0 Left for 0.1 mile to an unmarked road on the right.

42.1 Right for 3 miles to the end.

You'll pass a paper mill.

45.1 Left for 1.3 miles to an unmarked road on the right that comes up while you're going downhill.

46.4 Right for 1.2 miles to the end.

At the end, the main road turns left.

47.6 Left for 1.5 miles to the end (Route 167).

This is a glorious downhill run through large farms. At the end, Presque Isle is 3 miles to your left.

49.1 Right on Route 167 for 0.9 mile to Route 205 on the left.

There's a snack bar on the corner.

50.0 Left for about 11 miles to a crossroads and stop sign (Route 161).

This is a beautiful road following the Aroostook River, with rolling fields on both sides sloping down to the water.

61.0 Left on Route 161, crossing the river, for 0.3 mile to a traffic light (Route 1), in Caribou.

Caution: You cross railroad tracks just before the bridge. Also, watch out for the expansion joints as you cross the bridge.

61.3   To get to Days Inn, turn right on Route 1 for 1.3 miles to Route 89. The motel is on Route 89 just past the intersection. There's a restaurant at the motel.

   To get to Russell's Motel, go straight across Route 1 for 0.2 mile to end (South Main Street, Route 164), and turn left for 1.2 miles. Russell's Motel is on your left. To get to the Old Iron Inn (155 High Street), turn right on Route 1 for 0.5 mile, and left on High Street.
   Final mileage: 62.6.

Third Day: Caribou to Fort Kent (60 miles)

0.0   Head into the center of Caribou, which is on Route 161 ¼ mile west of Route 1. You will be heading northwest out of town on Route 161.

   The downtown area consists of several one-way roads which form a counterclockwise loop. Fortunately, Route 161 is well marked.

1.0   (Approximate mileage—the distance from the motels to downtown varies slightly.) From downtown, head out of town on Route 161 North for 8 miles to Capitol Hill Road, which bears right (a sign says "to New Sweden"). Route 161 turns several times as you leave downtown Caribou.

   You pass through wide open potato country.

9.0   Bear right on Capitol Hill Road for 0.7 mile to the end (Station Road).

   You'll pass a handsome concrete church built in 1871. At the end is the New Sweden Historical Museum, an attractive white building with a clock tower.

9.7   Left on Station Road for 0.6 mile to a crossroads and stop sign. (Route 161 again).

   There's a grocery on the corner.

10.3   Bear right on Route 161 for about 8 miles to Lake Shore Road, a small road on the left that parallels the main road. It's about a mile after the bottom of a long, fast descent.

18.4   Left for 1.4 miles to the end (Route 161 again).

   As soon as you turn onto the side road you'll see Madawaska Lake. The road runs along its shore.

19.8   Left on Route 161 for 8.4 miles to Route 162 on the right (a sign says "to Sinclair, Saint Agatha").

   There's a grocery shortly before the intersection in Guerette—it's the only building in town—and a snack bar at the intersection.

28.2   Right on Route 162 for 4 miles to the stop sign, in Sinclair. Route 162 turns left here.

32.2   Left (still Route 162) for about 13 miles to the end (Route 1).

   This is a delightful ride along the shore of Long Lake, passing cozy cottages and cabins. Wooded hills rise from the opposite shore. As you continue along the lake, the land opens up into large farms with big, weathered barns. Saint Agatha, at the far end of the lake, is a town of trim white houses spread out along the road, with a large, handsome brick church at the top of the hill. Beyond Saint Agatha, rolling potato fields descend to the Saint John River.

45.2 Left on Route 1 for about 12.5 miles to Route 11 on the left, in Fort Kent. **Caution:** There are three dangerous railroad crossings on this section—two after Upper Frenchville, and one as you come into Fort Kent at the bottom of a hill. Please dismount.

The road follows the Saint John River, which curves gently through a narrow valley with wooded hills on both sides. Shortly after turning onto Route 1 you'll go through Upper Frenchville, which, like Saint Agatha, is a small town dominated by an impressive Catholic church. The Fort Kent Blockhouse is on your right, about 100 yards off the road, just before Route 11. Daigle's Bed & Breakfast is on the left as you come into town, just past the hospital. Rock's Motel is on Route 1 shortly after the intersection with Route 11.

Final mileage: 57.7.

Fourth Day: Fort Kent to Ashland (50 miles)

Be sure to eat a hearty breakfast in Fort Kent, as the terrain will now become very hilly, and sources of food are few and far between.

0.0 Head south out of Fort Kent on Route 11 for about 50 miles to the crossroads where Route 11 turns right, in Ashland.

The road climbs a series of steplike hills to get out of Fort Kent. Beyond, the terrain is demanding, with vigorous ascents and delightful descents. You'll climb steeply onto a ridge with spectacular views of rolling hillsides and Eagle Lake in the distance, and then you will

Mount Katahdin rises dramatically across a field, Patten.

descend to the lake and follow its shore.

There's a grocery in Eagle Lake about 16 miles from Fort Kent; the next food is 22 miles ahead, in Portage (there's a motel here also). Beyond Eagle Lake the land is mostly wooded, with an occasional view from a ridge. There are several steep climbs before Portage.

Just before Ashland, Route 11 turns left across the Aroostook River and a smaller road goes straight. If you go straight for 0.3 mile, you'll come to the Ashland Logging Museum, which contains several buildings and sheds, and some massive felled trees. The hill into Ashland is a monster. As you're climbing it, look back for a great view.

50.0 Right at the crossroads in Ashland (still Route 11) for ¼ mile to Route 163 on the left.

50.2 Left for 0.2 mile to the Four Seasons Motel on the left. The motel has a restaurant.

Final mileage 50.4

Fifth Day: Ashland to Sherman (58 miles)

Again, eat heartily in Ashland, and stock up on groceries and liquids. There is no food on the 38-mile stretch between Masardis and Patten.

0.0 From the motel, backtrack 0.2 mile to Route 11.

0.2 Left on Route 11 for about 48 miles to Route 159 on the right as you come into Patten.

The road out of Ashland follows a high, mostly open ridge to the lumber-mill town of Masardis, 10 miles south. The grocery store here is the last source of food for 38 miles. Beyond Masardis is nearly unbroken woodland almost to Patten. The 17 miles between Route 212 and Patten are very hilly, with the worst climb a few miles before Patten.

48.2 Right on Route 159 for 0.3 mile to the Lumberman's Museum, and backtrack to Route 11.

48.8 Turn right on Route 11, continuing south. After about 9 miles Route 11 turns right, but continue straight to the Katahdin Valley Motel on the left.

There's a steep climb about a mile long when you leave Patten, but you'll be rewarded by magnificent views of Mount Katahdin, 25 miles away, on the right. There's a grocery in Sherman Station, about 2 miles from the end.

Final mileage: 58.

Author's note: I'd like to know how many riders take this tour. If you tackle it, could you please let me know? You can contact me in care of Backcountry Publications, P.O. Box 175, Woodstock, VT 05091.

Bicycle Repair Services

Aroostook Bicycle Company, Reach Road, Presque Isle (764-0206)
Bicycle Peddler, D. Daigle & Sons, 15 Market Street, Fort Kent (834-5060)

25.

The Linear Tour: Kittery to Bar Harbor and Back

Distance: About 240 miles each way.
Terrain: Generally rolling, with occasional difficult hills.
Special features: A continuous tour along the Maine coast using secondary roads wherever possible.

The tour from the southern tip of Maine up the coast to Bar Harbor, or from Bar Harbor down the coast to Kittery, is one of the most popular bicycling excursions in the East. Unfortunately, nearly every bicycle tourist follows Route 1 for all or most of the distance—a road which is at best boring and unattractive and at worst unsafe. Every time I've driven along Route 1 I've seen bicycle tourists, their bikes loaded with panniers and sleeping bags; but I've never seen a touring cyclist on the wealth of secondary roads that parallel Route 1, because many of these roads do not show up on the standard highway maps that most bicyclists use to plan their routes. The East Coast Bicycle Trail, a popular linear tour on back roads, runs from Virginia to Boston; northeast of Boston, the touring cyclist is on his or her own.

The tour starts from the bridge between Portsmouth, New Hampshire, and Kittery, Maine. For the most part, it follows the coast to Bar Harbor, using secondary roads whenever possible. The route is fairly direct, except for a slight semicircle to the west that bypasses Portland. The northbound and southbound routes are the same except for about a quarter of the tour where, for variety, the southbound route runs further inland.

Food stores, restaurants, and accommodations are plentiful on the tour; and the choice is yours. In nearly every coastal town you'll find motels, inns, and Bed and Breakfasts. Campgrounds, indicated by a triangle on the maps, occur along or very close to the route at least every 30 miles. Lists of accommodations and campgrounds may be obtained from the Maine Publicity Bureau, 97 Winthrop Street, Hallowell, Maine 04347. During the off-season, indoor accommodations are inexpensive and usually do not fill up. During the summer, the opposite situation prevails; it's a good idea to set an end-of-day goal each morning, call an accommodation there, and reserve a spot. If it is full, often an innkeeper will call other places nearby (especially if you explain that you're on a bicycle tour), and you can call back in a few minutes to see if another spot was found. Personally I prefer to camp on bicycle tours and avoid the daily hassle of finding indoor accommodations.

Because the tour is long, I have kept the descriptions of points of interest brief, or have referred to other tours in the book where the place is described in more detail. The map is divided into sections, because it is obviously impossible to put the entire tour on one sheet of paper.

Linear A: Kittery to Bar Harbor

Most cyclists enter Maine from Portsmouth, New Hampshire, on Route 1, crossing the most easterly of the three bridges between Portsmouth and Kittery. From the Boston–Brookline–Cambridge–Somerville area, the best bicycle route to Portsmouth is to cross the Route 99 bridge into Everett. Go two-thirds of the way around the rotary at Route 16 onto Main Street, heading due north. Follow Main Street through Malden, Melrose, Wakefield (where Main Street becomes Haverhill Street when you cross Route 128 at the rotary), and North Reading. At the end, bear left on Route 114 (there is camping nearby at Harold Parker State Forest) for about 3 miles to Route 125 North on the right. Follow Route 125 to Haverhill. Continue north on Route 108 to Exeter, New Hampshire. (There is a campground 1.1 miles south of town.) Beyond Exeter, bear right on Route 101 to Route 1 in Portsmouth, and turn left on Route 1.

From Boston's western suburbs, pick up Route 62, follow it northeast to Route 28, turn left for about 2 miles to Route 125 North, and follow it to Haverhill.

0.0 From the bridge on Route 1 between New Hampshire and Maine, go 0.4 mile to the traffic island where Route 1 curves left.

0.4 Go straight along the right side of the island for 50 feet to the end, and turn right for 0.3 mile to the traffic light, in the center of Kittery.

0.7 Straight onto Route 103. Follow it for 8 miles to the end (Route 1A), in York Harbor.

Historic York Village is ½ mile to the left on Route 1A (see Ride 1).

8.7 Right on Route 1A for 3.5 miles to Nubble Road, which bears right uphill, following the ocean.

12.2 Bear right on Nubble Road. After ½ mile the main road curves right, following the water. Continue for 0.4 mile to a fork where Sohier Park Road bears right.

13.1 Bear right for 0.1 mile to the dead end, enjoy the view of Cape Neddick Light (also called Nubble Light), and backtrack 0.1 mile to the main road.

13.3 Right for 0.6 mile to Kendall Road on the right, after Forthill Avenue.

13.9 Right for ½ mile to the stop sign.

Caution: There is a steep, winding downhill shortly after you turn onto Kendall Road.

14.4 Turn right at the stop sign, following the ocean, for 0.3 mile to the end

(Route 1A), in the center of York Beach.

14.7 Right for 0.6 mile to a fork where Route 1A bears left and Shore Road goes straight.

> **Caution:** Shore Road, which you will take to Ogunquit, is very narrow, very curvy, and, on beach days, very busy. When busy, there is not enough room for a car to pass a bicycle safely without either risking a head-on collision or squeezing the cyclist off the road. If the traffic looks bad, it's safer to bear left on Route 1A to Route 1, and turn right on Route 1 to Ogunquit.

15.3 Straight on Shore Road for 4.8 miles to a small road which turns sharply right at a stop sign and traffic island. The main road curves left at the intersection. A sign in the traffic island says "Perkins Cove."

20.1 Sharp right for 0.3 mile to the tip of the small peninsula bordering Perkins Cove and backtrack to Shore Road.

> Marginal Way (see Ride 2) is worth exploring.

20.7 Bear right for 1 mile to the end (merge right on Route 1), in the center of Ogunquit.

> The beach is ¼ mile to the right.

21.7 Bear right on Route 1 (there's no escaping it in places) for 1.8 miles to Bourne Avenue on the right, at a traffic light. It's immediately after the Wells-Moody Motel on the right.

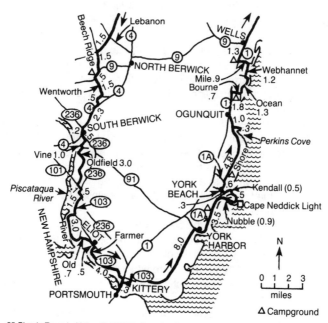

25 Bicycle Tours in Maine © 1986 Backcountry Publications

23.5 Right on Bourne Avenue for 0.7 mile to the end.

24.2 Left along the ocean for 1.3 miles to Webhannet Drive on the right.

25.5 Right, following the ocean, for 1.2 miles to the end.

26.7 Left for 0.9 mile to the end (Route 1).

27.6 Right for about 6 miles to the traffic light (Water Street on the right) as you come into downtown Kennebunk, immediately after the bridge.

> **Caution:** For the first three miles, Route 1 is a busy 3-lane road with no shoulder. Keep to the right. There are several campgrounds between Wells and Route 9. Of interest are the Wells Auto Museum and the Brick Store Museum in Kennebunk (0.2 mile north of the traffic light—see Ride 3).

33.6 Left at the light for 0.4 mile to the end (merge left on Route 35 at the stop sign).

34.0 Bear left for 1.4 mile to the fork, just after the bridge over the Maine Turnpike, where one road goes straight and the other road (Route 35) bears right.

> The Turnpike Motel is just before the fork.

35.4 Straight (don't bear right on Route 35) for 3 miles to a fork where the main road bears right, and Old Falls Road bears left.

> You'll pass Yankeeland Campground and Mousam River Campground, good spots away from the beach traffic, on the left.

38.4 Bear right on the main road for 2.4 miles to the end (merge right).

40.8 Bear right for 100 yards to Route 35 North on the left.

40.9 Left for about 32 miles to Route 302, at a traffic light in the center of North Windham.

> **Caution:** The metal-grate bridge across the Saco River, after about 18 miles, is very slippery when wet; it's safest to walk across. The Daniel Marrett House in Standish, built in 1789, is open to the public.

71.0 Straight at the traffic light onto Route 115 for 3 miles to the end (Routes 202 and 4).

74.0 Left (still Route 115) for 3.8 miles to the traffic light in the center of Gray.

77.8 Continue straight on Route 115 (don't bear left on Routes 202 and 4) for 1.6 miles to a road that bears left (a sign says "to Pineland Center").

79.4 Bear left for 2.8 miles to the end (Route 231).

82.2 Left for 100 yards to a crossroads (Pownal Depot Road on the right).

> On the left is Pineland Center, a state institution for the severely handicapped.

82.3 Right for 1.8 miles to the second right, at the top of the steep hill.

84.1 Right for 2.4 miles to a crossroads and stop sign (Route 9).

> If you turn left on Route 9 for ½ mile you'll come to Bradbury Mountain State Park, where a trail leads ¼ mile to the top of a hill with a sweeping view. Just beyond the picnic area is the park campground, on the right.

86.5 Cross Route 9 and go 4.5 miles to Routes 125 and 136 on the right.

91.0 Right for 0.6 mile to the end (Route 1).

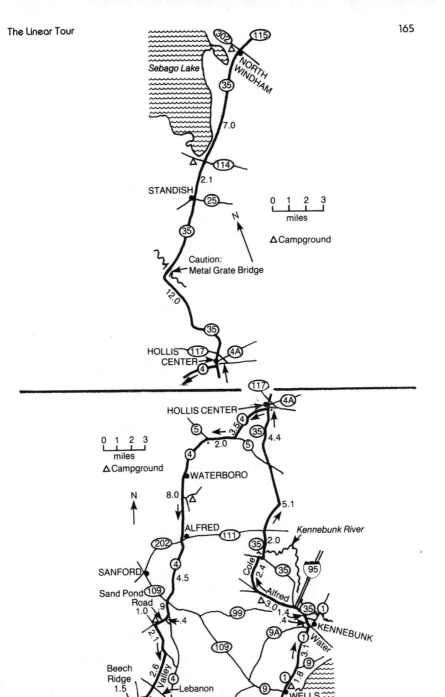

91.6 Right for 0.3 mile to Bow Street on the left, opposite L.L. Bean.

91.9 Left for 1.6 miles to a fork where Pleasant Hill Road bears left.

93.5 Bear left for 4.4 miles to a diagonal crossroads, at a "Yield" sign.

97.9 Straight for 1.8 miles to the end.

99.7 Left for 1.2 miles to Route 24 South, which bears right immediately before a large, Gothic wooden church on the right.

> This is the center of Brunswick. Just before the intersection you'll pass Bowdoin College on the right (see Ride 5).The Bowdoin College Museum of Art and the Peary-MacMillan Arctic Museum are excellent.

100.9 Bear right on Route 24 for 2.4 miles to the traffic light where Route 24 turns right (shopping center on corner).

103.3 Straight for 4.8 miles to the end (merge right on Route 1).

108.1 Bear right for ½ mile to a ramp which bears right downhill (a sign says "to business district").

> **Caution:** The road is very busy.

108.6 Bear right to the traffic light at the bottom, and straight onto another ramp onto the long bridge across the Kennebec River (Route 1 again).

> Downtown Bath and the Maine Maritime Museum, to the left at the stop sign, are worth visiting (see Ride 5).

108.8 Cross the bridge. (It's safest to use the sidewalk if traffic is heavy.) At the far end, continue for 0.4 mile to Route 127 on the left.

109.6 Left for 4 miles to the third right, which is unmarked. It's just after the second right, which is a short dead-end road.

113.6 Right (this is Old Stage Road) for 3.5 miles to the end (merge left at the stop sign).

117.1 Bear left for 0.2 mile to a fork.

117.3 Bear right for 1.5 miles to the end (again, merge left at the stop sign).

118.8 Bear left for 0.8 mile to the end (Route 1).

119.6 Left for 0.8 mile to Route 218 on the left, in the center of Wiscasset.

> Of interest are the Nickels-Sortwell House (1807), Castle Tucker (also 1807), and the Musical Wonder House. (See Ride 7 for more detail.)

120.4 Left on Route 218 for 4.4 miles to a road on the right opposite a small electric substation.

> After 0.3 mile, the Lincoln County Museum and Old Jail (1811) will be on the right.

124.8 Right for 4 miles to the end (Route 1), passing through Sheepscot.

128.8 Left for 0.8 mile to the first right (a sign says "to Newcastle, River Road").

129.6 Right for 1 mile to the intersection where Business Route 1 curves right and Route 215 goes straight, in Newcastle.

130.6 Curve right on Business Route 1 for 2 miles to Back Meadow Road, which bears right.

> The intersection is 0.6 mile after a supermarket on the right. You'll go through downtown Damariscotta and by the Chapman-Hall House (1754).

132.6 Bear right on Back Meadow Road. After 1.1 miles the main road curves sharply left. Continue for 1.8 miles to a wide crossroads (Route 1).

135.5 Right for 5 miles to a road that bears right at a small traffic island after the ''Welcome to Waldoboro'' sign.

> This section of Route 1 has a wide shoulder.

140.5 Right for 2.3 miles to Route 1 again, at a traffic light.

> There's a long descent into Waldoboro followed by a long climb out of it. At the top of the hill, the main road curves left at a fork. The Waldoboro Historical Society Museum is on the left just before Route 1 (see Ride 9). Moody's Diner, a great food stop, is on the right when you get to Route 1.

142.8 Right on Route 1 for 0.9 mile to Route 235 on the left.

143.7 Left for 4.4 miles to the second crossroads, which is 0.6 mile beyond the first one.

148.1 Right for 4.2 miles to a crossroads and stop sign (Route 90).

152.3 Straight for 0.1 mile to the first left.

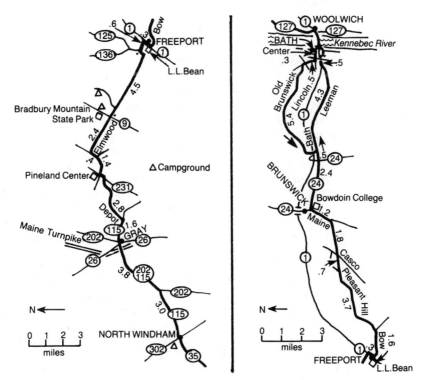

152.4 Left for 1 mile to the end (Route 131).

There's a steep drop into Warren and a tough climb out.

153.4 Left for 0.2 mile to the crossroads (Route 90 again).

153.6 Right for 6.7 miles to a traffic light (Route 17).

160.3 Cross Route 17 and go 2.8 miles to Route 1, at another light.

163.1 Cross Route 1 and go 0.2 mile to the end.

163.3 Left for 0.3 mile to the end, on the far side of the bridge, in Rockport.

163.6 Right for 0.2 mile to the intersection at the top of the hill, where the main road bears right and another road turns left. (A sign for the road on the left says "to Camden".)

163.8 Bear right for 1 mile to Bayview Street on the right.

If you turn right after 0.4 mile on Calderwood Lane and go 0.7 mile, Vesper Hill Chapel (see Ride 11) will be on the right.

164.8 Right on Bayview Street for 1.7 miles to the end (merge right on Route 1), in the center of Camden.

166.5 Bear right for 0.2 mile to the fork where Route 1 bears right and Route 52 bears left.

For a side trip to Mount Battie, bear right on Route 1 for 1.5 miles, and left into Camden Hills State Park (campground here also) for 1.3 miles to the summit. (See Ride 11.)

166.7 Bear left on Route 52 for about 17 miles, through lovely rolling farmland, to Route 1, on the outskirts of Belfast.

After 7 miles, Route 52 turns right at a crossroads.

183.7 Left on Route 1 for about 28 miles to Route 176 on the right, approximately 8 miles beyond Bucksport.

This section of Route 1 has a good shoulder (except for the bridges in Belfast and Bucksport), fine views of Penobscot Bay, and several campgrounds. After about 7 miles, in Searsport, is the excellent Penobscot Marine Museum, housed in a group of six buildings. If you bear left on Route 174 immediately before the first suspension bridge, just ahead is Fort Knox, a fascinating spot with ramparts, turrets, narrow corridors, and some of its original cannon. It was built in 1844 after the Aroostook War, a bloodless border dispute with Canada.

211.7 Right on Route 176 for about 9 miles to the end (Route 172), at a stop sign. This is the village of Surry.

220.7 Left on Route 172 for about 6.5 miles to the end (merge right on Routes 1 and 3). **Caution:** The intersection comes up while you're going downhill.

Just before the end, set back from the road on a large tract of land, is the Black House, an opulent Federal-era mansion built in 1826. The name refers to the family that owned it, not the color.

227.2 Bear right on Routes 1 and 3 for 0.3 mile to the traffic light (Route 230 on the right). **Caution:** Steep descent.

Here the tour turns right, but if you want the services of the Ellsworth commercial strip (motels, shopping mall, fast food, etc.), continue

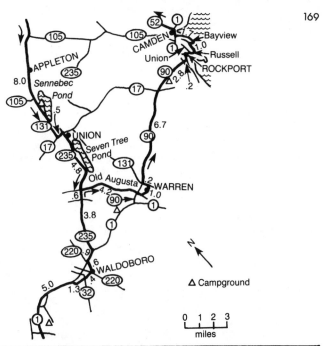

25 Bicycle Tours in Maine © 1986 Backcountry Publications

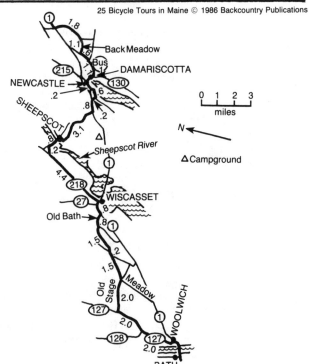

along Route 3 directly to Mount Desert Island, The strip is a four-lane, shoulderless highway extending for about a mile.

227.5 Right on Route 230 for 1.7 miles to Beechland Road on the left.

Here the tour turns left, but if you'd prefer a scenic, low-traffic alternative route which is 5.5 miles longer, continue straight on Route 230 for about 12.5 miles to the end (Route 3), just before the bridge to Mount Desert Island. You can cut off 5 miles by bearing left off Route 230 after about 4.5 miles onto a dirt road, following it for 1.8 miles to the end, and turning left on Route 130 again to Route 3 (see map #10).

229.2 Left on Beechland Road for 0.9 mile to a busy crossroads (Route 3) and stop sign.

230.1 Right for about 7.5 miles to the fork where Route 3 bears left and Route 102 goes straight, just beyond the bridge to Mount Desert Island.

At the intersection is Barcadia Campground, a conveniently located spot. Route 3 is very heavily traveled, but there is a good shoulder.

237.6 Straight on Route 102 for 2.2 miles to Crooked Road on the left. It's 100 yards after the Town Hill Country Store on the left.

239.8 Turn 90 degrees left on Crooked Road (don't turn sharp left on Knox Road), and go 4.9 miles to the end (Route 3).

244.7 Right for 0.4 mile to the entrance to the Acadia National Park Visitor Center on the right.

If you want to head into Bar Harbor, continue as follows instead of fighting the traffic on Route 3. (For the Nova Scotia ferry terminal, continue on Route 3 for 1.5 miles.)

245.1 From the Visitor Center, turn right (south) and get on Park Loop Road. Go 1.8 miles to the first left (a sign says "to Bar Harbor").

There's a sweeping view of Frenchman Bay from the top of the hill beyond the Visitor Center.

246.9 Left for 0.8 mile to Route 3. Turn right on Route 3, and take the first left on Cottage Street into downtown Bar Harbor.

The Bar Harbor Bicycle Shop is at the corner of Route 3 and Cottage Street.

Final mileage: 247.7

Linear B: Bar Harbor to Kittery

The southbound tour follows the same route as the northbound tour for about three-quarters of its length. The other quarter runs parallel to the northbound tour, but further inland. For the sake of conciseness, I have not repeated descriptions of points of interest along the northbound route.

Start from the junction of Route 3 and West Street in Bar Harbor, at the northwest edge of town. The intersection is one block north of the Bar Harbor Bicycle Shop.

0.0 Bear left on West Street Extension, heading west, for 0.8 mile to the end (Park Loop Road).

0.8 Right for 1.8 miles to the crossroads immediately before the Visitor Center parking lot, and right for 100 yards to the end (Route 3).

2.7 Left for 0.4 mile to Crooked Road on the left, opposite Hulls Cove.

3.1 Turn left (**Caution** here). After 3.7 miles Gilbert Farm Road bears right, but continue straight on Crooked Road for 1.2 miles to the end (Route 102).

8.0 Right for 2.2 miles to the end (Route 3).

10.2 Left (**Caution** here) for about 7.5 miles to a crossroads (Beechland Road on the left, Buttermilk Road on the right).

> For a more scenic, lightly traveled alternative route which is 5.5 miles longer, turn left after 1.3 miles onto Route 230 and follow it for about 14 miles to Route 1 in Ellsworth. You can cut off about 5 miles by turning right off Route 230 after 1.5 miles onto a dirt road, following it for 1.8 miles to the end, and bearing right on Route 130 again (see the map).

17.7 Left on Beechland Road (**Caution** here) for 0.9 mile to the end (Route 230).

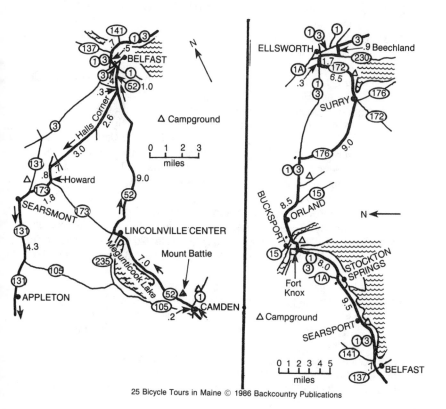

25 Bicycle Tours in Maine © 1986 Backcountry Publications

18.6 Right for 1.7 miles to Route 1 at the traffic light in Ellsworth.

20.3 Left for 0.3 mile to Route 172, which bears left while you're climbing a steep hill.

20.6 Bear left for about 6.5 miles to Route 176 on the right, just past the village of Surry. At the beginning of Route 172, you'll pass the Black House on the right.

27.1 Right on Route 176 for about 9 miles to the end (Route 1).

36.1 Left on Route 1 for about 28 miles to Route 52, in Belfast.

> This section of Route 1 has a good shoulder (except for the bridges in Bucksport and Belfast). The Penobscot Marine Museum is located in Searsport.

64.1 Right on Route 52 for 1.3 miles to an unmarked road which bears right, at a fork. (It's the second right.)

> There's a country store at the intersection.

65.4 Bear right. After 2.6 miles bear slightly right at a fork, staying on the main road. (The Belmont town line is just ahead.) Continue for 3 miles to a crossroads and stop sign.

71.0 Straight for 0.7 mile to the end (merge left at a stop sign).

71.7 Bear left. After 0.8 mile you'll merge head-on into Route 173. Continue straight for 1.8 miles to the end (Route 131).

74.3 Left for about 12.5 miles to the end (Route 17), passing through magnificent rolling countryside.

> There are groceries in Searsmont and Appleton.

86.8 Left on Route 17 for ½ mile to Route 235 on the right, at a stop sign.

> Elmer's Restaurant, on the left at the intersection, is a good food stop.

87.3 Right on Route 235 for about 9 miles to the end (Route 1).

> After ¼ mile you'll go through Union, a lovely New England town built around a large, sloping green (see Ride 9). **Caution:** In Union, a crossroads and stop sign come up suddenly while you're going downhill. Beyond Union, you'll follow Seven Tree Pond on your left. Look back over your left shoulder for views of the Camden Hills across the pond.

96.3 Right on Route 1 for 0.9 mile to a crossroads (Route 220).

> Moody's Diner, on the left at the intersection, is a great food stop.

97.2 Turn left on Route 220. After 0.6 mile, Route 220 turns left while you're going down a steep hill, but continue straight for 1.6 miles to the end (Route 1 again).

> There's a long, fairly steep climb up to Route 1.

99.4 Left on Route 1 for about 5 miles to a crossroads (Black Meadow Road turns left; a sign says "to Lake Pemaquid Campground").

> The road on the left goes up a short, steep hill. This section of Route 1 has a good shoulder.

104.4 Left at crossroads for 1.8 miles to a fork where the main road bears right.

106.2 Bear right for 1.1 mile to the end (Business Route 1).

107.3 Turn left. After 2.1 miles the main road curves sharply left, shortly after downtown Damariscotta. Continue for 0.2 mile to a smaller road that bears left as you start to go uphill.

109.6 Bear left for 0.6 mile to a fork.

110.2 Bear right for 0.2 mile to the end (Route 1).

110.4 Left for 0.8 mile to the first right, which goes up a short hill.

111.2 Turn right. After 3.1 miles the main road curves 90 degrees left as you come into Sheepscot. Continue for 0.8 mile to a fork.

115.1 Bear left for 0.2 mile to the end (Route 218).

115.3 Left for 4.4 miles to the crossroads (Route 1) and stop sign in Wiscasset. Shortly before the end, the Lincoln County Museum and Old Jail is on the left. For other historic buildings, see Ride 7.

119.7 Right for 0.8 mile to Old Bath Road on the right, after Bradford Road.

120.5 Right for 0.8 mile to a fork, where a smaller road bears right.

121.3 Bear right for 1.5 miles to the end (merge left at the stop sign).

122.8 Bear slightly left for 0.2 mile to the fork, 100 yards after the cemetery on the right.

123.0 Bear right at the fork (don't turn right immediately after the cemetery). Go 1.5 miles to another fork where the main road bears right.

124.5 Bear right for 2 miles to the end (Route 127).

126.5 Left for 4 miles to the end (Route 1).

130.5 Right for 1 mile to the first right on the far side of the bridge (Front Street), in Bath.

It's safest to use the sidewalk on the left side of the bridge.

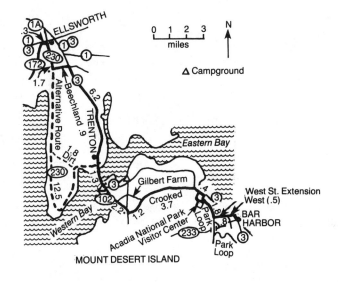

MOUNT DESERT ISLAND

131.5 Right for 1 block to the first left (Centre Street), opposite the town hall.
The Maine Maritime Museum (see Ride 6) is worth visiting.

131.6 Left for 0.3 mile to Lincoln Street on the right, at the top of the hill, immediately after the red brick courthouse on the left.
Lincoln Street is just after High Street, the crossroads at the top of the hill.

131.9 Right on Lincoln Street for ½ mile to a crossroads with a combined gas station and grocery on the corner.

132.4 Go straight at the crossroads, and then immediately bear left on Old Brunswick Road for 5.4 miles to the end, at a traffic light.

137.8 Right for ½ mile to another traffic light.
There's a shopping center on the far left corner.

138.3 Straight on Route 24 for 2.2 miles to another traffic light (Route 123 on the left).

140.5 Straight for 0.2 mile to the stop sign immediately after the large, Gothic-style church, in the center of Brunswick.
You'll pass Bowdoin College on the left (see Ride 5).

140.7 Left for 1.3 miles to Pleasant Hill Road, which bears right just past the hospital on the left.
At the beginning of this stretch, Bowdoin College will again be on your left.

142.0 Bear right on Pleasant Hill Road for 1.8 miles to a diagonal crossroads.

143.8 Straight for 4.4 miles to the end (merge right at the "Yield" sign).

148.2 Bear right for 1.6 miles to the end (Route 1).
L.L. Bean is in front of you.

149.8 Right for 0.3 mile to Route 125 on the left (a sign says "to I-95").

150.1 Left for 0.6 mile to the end (Route 125 turns right).

150.7 Left for 4.5 miles to the crossroads and stop sign (Route 9).
If you turn right for ½ mile you'll come to Bradbury Mountain State Park where a trail leads ¼ mile to the top of a hill with a panoramic view. A campground is just past the picnic area.

155.2 Cross Route 9 and go 2.4 miles to the end.

157.6 Left for 1.8 miles to a crossroads (Route 231) and stop sign.
Pineland Center, a state institution for the severely handicapped, is on the far side of the intersection.

159.4 Turn left on Route 231 for 100 yards, and bear right on Gray Depot Road for 2.8 miles to the end (Route 115). **Caution:** There are railroad tracks at the bottom of a steep hill.

162.3 Right on Route 115 for 1.6 miles to the traffic light, in the center of Gray.

163.9 Straight (still Route 115, also Routes 202 and 4), for 3.8 miles to the point where Route 115 bears right.

167.7 Bear right (still Route 115) for 3 miles to Route 302 at the traffic light in the center of North Windham.

170.7 Go straight at the light onto Route 35. Follow Route 35 for about 22 miles to Route 4, at a stop sign.

Caution: After about 14 miles, you'll come to the metal grate bridge over the Saco River. The bridge is very slippery when wet. It's safest to walk across.

193.0 Right on Route 4 for about 18 miles to Route 109, at a traffic light.

211.0 Continue straight on Route 4 for 0.9 mile to Country Club Road 2, which bears right.

211.9 Bear right for 0.4 mile to a fork where Sand Pond Road bears right. You'll pass a campground.

212.3 Bear right for 1 mile to a crossroads and stop sign.

213.3 Left for 2.1 miles to Valley Road (unmarked) on the right.

215.4 Right for 2.6 miles to a crossroads and stop sign (Lebanon Street on the left). It's the second paved crossroads.

218.0 Straight for 1.5 miles to the next crossroads (Beech Ridge Road).

219.5 Left for 1.5 miles to the end (merge right on Route 9).

The author, with Portland Head Light, Cape Elizabeth, in the background.

221.0 Bear right for ½ mile to Wentworth Road on the left, shortly after the camp-ground.

221.5 Left for 1.5 miles to the end.

223.0 Right for ½ mile to the end (Route 4).

223.5 Right for 2.3 miles to the end, where Route 4 turns left, in South Berwick. On the right at the intersection is the Georgian house of the writer Sarah Orne Jewett, built in 1774.

225.8 Left (still Route 4) for 0.2 mile to Route 236 on the left.

226.0 Left for ½ mile to Vine Street on the right.

226.5 Right for 1 mile to the end (Oldfield Road on the right).

227.5 Right for 3 miles to the end (Route 101). As soon as you turn, the Hamilton House, an elegant Georgian mansion with extensive grounds along the Salmon Falls River, is on the right, set back from the road. Just past the mansion is the Vaughan Woods Memorial, a lovely picnic area along the river.

230.5 Left on Route 101 for 0.1 mile to the diagonal crossroads and stop sign (Route 236).

230.6 Bear right for ½ mile to Route 103 on the right.

231.1 Right for 1.5 miles to River Road on the right, shortly after a small bridge over an inlet.

232.6 Right on River Road for 3 miles to Old Road, which bears right at a traffic island. (A sign may also say River Road.)

235.6 Bear right for 0.7 mile to the end, at the Eliot town green (merge slightly right on Route 103).

236.3 Bear right for ½ mile to Moses Gerrish Farmer Road (also Route 103) on the right.

236.8 Right (still Route 103) for 3.2 miles to the end (Dennett Road), at a stop sign.

240.0 Right (still Route 103) for 0.7 mile to Route 1, at the traffic light. You're in Kittery. Route 103 bears right and left several times, but it is well marked.

240.7 Right on Route 1 for ½ mile to the bridge to Portsmouth, New Hampshire. Final mileage: 241.2.

Bicycle Repair Services

Goodrich's Bicycle Shop, 111 School Street, Sanford (324-1381)
Power & Motion, 46 Cottage Street, Sanford (324-7853)
Frost & Flame, Route 115, North Windham (892-3070)
Birgfeld Bicycle Shop, Route 1, Searsport (548-2916)
The Spokesperson, Springvale Commons, Springvale (324-5426)
Also consult bike shop listings for Tours 1-15 and 19.